DEVOTIONS
FOR
Little Boys and Girls

New Testament

by Joan C. Webb

art by Joanne Vavrek McCallum

Library of Congress Cataloging-in-Publication Data

Webb, Joan C., 1948-
    Devotions for little boys and girls / by Joan C. Webb : art by
Joanne Vavrek McCallum.
        p.   cm.
    Contents: [1] New Testament — [2] Old Testament.
    ISBN 0-87403-682-8
    1. Bible—Devotional use—Juvenile literature. 2. Children—
Prayer-books and devotions—English. 3. Bible games and puzzles—
Juvenile literature. 4. Devotional calendars—Juvenile literature.
    [1. Prayer books and devotions.] I. McCallum, Jodie, ill.
II. Title.
BS617.8.W43 1992
242'.62—dc20   91-37705
                                                      CIP
                                                      AC

Table of Contents

Dear Parents,

When my son and daughter were young, I searched for a book that I could read to them each night. I wanted the book to have short, simple stories based on biblical concepts. I wanted contemporary illustrations for the stories; pictures the children could identify with. My desire was to help them learn how the God-given truths of the Bible related to their lives. Although I did not find exactly what I wanted, I continued to read and adapt the existing books and stories to our family's specific needs.

Devotions for Little Boys and Girls is an outgrowth of my original search. It is a daily Bible story devotional book for you and your child. It is designed to help you, the parent, guide your child in understanding God's love for him or her through His Son, Jesus, and His written Word, the Bible. Each story begins with a verse to think about and concludes with follow-up in the form of questions, suggested activities, and a prayer. Many of the simple activities encourage quiet learning times with your child. For active interaction, perhaps the following day, you may wish to do the more involved suggested activities.

This book is intended for young children three to six years old. Each devotion is complete on one page. You may write your child's name on the blank provided within the devotion. In this way, the book becomes uniquely individual. To encourage further participation, you may have your child draw a happy face or place a sticker at the top of the page to celebrate completing each story and/or activity (suggested stickers, Happy Heart Miniatures-#22-01375 or Children's Face Miniatures-#22-01386 by Standard Publishing).

I recommend that you hold or touch your child as you read to him or her, making this daily time a loving, sharing experience. Have fun!

Joan C. Webb

SURPRISED BY AN ANGEL
LUKE 1:5-22

But God has listened. He has heard my prayer. *Psalm 66:19*

_____, there once was a husband and wife who wanted a baby very much. The husband, Zechariah, was a priest-leader in the Temple-church. Elizabeth was his wife. Both Zechariah and Elizabeth loved God. Year after year they asked God for a baby. They were old enough to be grandparents, but still they had no children.

One day when Zechariah was in the Temple an angel of God came to him. Zechariah was so surprised by the angel that he was afraid.

"Don't be afraid, Zechariah," said the angel. "I have good news that will make you very happy. God has heard your prayers all these years. It's the right time now. Elizabeth is going to have a baby boy. Name him John. God has a special job for John to do."

But then Zechariah said to the angel, "That can't be, my wife and I are too old to have a baby."

"Oh, yes, it's true. I am giving you a message from God," the angel answered. "But you, Zechariah, because you didn't believe, will lose your voice until the day your son, John, is born."

God always hears us when we pray. Sometimes, though, it isn't the right time for the answer that we want. Zechariah and Elizabeth waited and prayed a long time for a baby. Finally, God said, "It's time. Now you will be the parents of a very special son."

Questions:
1. What did Zechariah and Elizabeth want? (a baby)
2. What did the angel say? (Don't be afraid. I have good news.)

Activity:
Wrap your child in a white sheet or blanket and have him pretend to give the good news (like the angel did) to Zechariah.

Prayer:
Dear God, You heard Zechariah and Elizabeth's prayers. When it was the right time, You said, "Yes." I believe You hear me when I pray, even though I don't always get the answer in the time I want. Amen.

WHO'S TALKING TO MARY?
LUKE 1:26-38

But God can do all things. *Matthew 19:26*

_____, angels are God's special message givers. The same angel who told Zechariah about his baby son also came to a young woman named Mary.

Mary was going to be married soon. Her husband-to-be was Joseph. While Mary was busy thinking and planning for her wedding, the angel, Gabriel, came to talk to Mary. "Hello, Mary," he said. "God is happy with you. And He is with you."

Mary looked at the angel. She was confused. She wondered, "Why is this angel saying these things? I do not understand."

But Gabriel said, "Don't be afraid, Mary. God has a wonderful plan for you. Listen! You are going to have a baby son. His name will be Jesus. He will be great. He will be called the Son of God. No other person will ever be like Him."

Then Mary asked, "But how can I have a baby? I'm not married to Joseph yet. We don't live together."

Gabriel said, "God has a special plan. He will be Jesus' Father. Only God can make this plan work."

So Mary believed the angel's words. She said, "I am God's woman. I will do whatever He wants. I know all God's promises will come true." Mary was right. God's promises always come true.

Questions:
1. Who came to Mary when she was planning her wedding? (angel)
2. What did the angel say? (You will have a baby who will be called the Son of God.)

Activity:
Whisper a promise to your child (ideas: We will take a walk. You can hold the baby today.). Ask him to whisper a promise to you.

Prayer:
Dear God, thank You that Mary believed Your promise would come true. Thank You that she wanted to have Jesus, Your Son. Amen.

8

HIS VOICE IS BACK
LUKE 1:57-64

We can trust God to do what he promised. *Hebrews 10:23*

_____, the day you were born was a very happy day. Grandma and Grandpa, your cousins, aunts and uncles were all so excited for us. The neighbors sent cards and gifts. It was a special time.

Many years ago when Elizabeth had baby John, the same thing happened. Friends and family were excited and happy for Elizabeth and Zechariah. When gifts arrived, the cards were written to Baby Zechariah. But Elizabeth said, "Oh, no, we are calling our baby John."

All the friends and family turned to look at each other. "Why?" they said. "We always name our boy babies after their fathers. How can his name be John?" Then they made hand and finger signs to voiceless Zechariah. "What do you want to name him?" they asked.

So Zechariah wrote these words: "His name is John." When Zechariah wrote down those words, his voice came back, just as the angel had promised. The people were very surprised. They wondered what this all meant.

"Thank You, God," prayed Zechariah. "You kept your promise to Elizabeth and me and have given us a son. I praise You. You are good."

Zechariah believed God had a special plan for his son, John. "You will grow up to be a messenger of God," Zechariah said. "You will help people to believe in God and to know that Jesus is God's Son."

Questions:

1. What did people want to name the baby boy? (Zechariah)

2. When did Zechariah get his voice back? (When he said, "His name is John.")

Activity:

Talk about why names are important. ("John" means "God is gracious.") If you know what your child's name means, tell him, or tell how you decided on his name.

Prayer

Dear God, thank You for keeping Your promises to Elizabeth and Zechariah. I know You'll always keep Your promises to me. Amen.

SH-H-H! THE BABY'S SLEEPING
LUKE 2:1-7

She will give birth to a son. You will name the son Jesus.
Matthew 1:21

_____, do you like babies? Sometimes we have to be quiet when a baby sleeps, don't we? Listen to a story about the night a very special baby was born.

Mary and Joseph had just arrived in the town of Bethlehem after a very long trip. They were tired and needed rest. Mary was going to have a baby. They looked all around the city for somewhere to stay for the night. But everywhere they went they were told, "Sorry, we have no rooms left."

Finally, someone felt sorry for Mary and Joseph and let them sleep in a crowded barn-like place with the animals. Joseph made it as comfortable as he could for Mary.

That night Mary had her baby, a beautiful baby boy. This special baby was different from all other babies. This baby was God's own Son. God told Mary and Joseph to name His Son Jesus. We now celebrate Jesus' birthday each year at Christmas time.

On that special night long ago, maybe the cows and chickens made noises while baby Jesus was trying to sleep. Maybe Mary said to them, "Sh-h-h . . . the baby's sleeping."

Questions:
1. Who is God's Son? (Jesus)
2. When do we celebrate Jesus' birthday? (Christmas time)

Activities:
1. Sing "Happy Birthday" to Jesus together with your child, even though it may not be the Christmas season.
2. Make the sounds that cows and chickens make.

Prayer:
Dear God, thank You for Mary and Joseph and that they took care of baby Jesus. Thank You for my mom and dad that that they take care of me, too. Amen.

A CHOIR IN THE SKY
LUKE 2:8-20

Don't be afraid, because I am bringing you some good news.

Luke 2:10

_____, remember the story about the night baby Jesus was born? That same night, a big choir of angels came to some shepherds in a field. They had a wonderful message for the shepherds.

When the shepherds saw the angels they were afraid. They did not know who the angels were. They did not know why the angels came to them. But then one of the angels said, "Do not be afraid, I have good news for all of you. Today in the town of Bethlehem a baby is born. He is Christ the Lord. Look for the baby wrapped tightly in blankets, lying in a little bed."

Then all at once, the big choir of angels started singing. It was a beautiful sound.

After the angels left, the shepherds said to each other, "Let's go see the baby that the angels have told us about." Quickly they started to walk to find Jesus. They walked and walked until they came to the barn-like place with all the animals. They found baby Jesus sleeping in a little bed, just as the angels promised. The shepherds bowed down and thanked God for His Son, Jesus.

You and I can bow down and thank God for Jesus, too.

Questions:

1. What did the angel say to the shepherd? (I have good news for you. A baby is born today.)

2. Where did the shepherds find Jesus? (sleeping in a little bed)

Activities:

1. Draw a picture of baby Jesus wrapped in the blankets.

2. Bow down on your knees with your child to pray.

Prayer:

Dear God, thank You for the singing angels that brought the good news about Jesus' birth. Thank You for the shepherds. And most of all, thank You for baby Jesus. Amen.

WHO'S HOLDING BABY JESUS?
LUKE 2:25-35

Then Simeon took the baby in his arms and thanked God. *Luke 2:28*

_____, do you like secrets?

A long time ago there was an old man, named Simeon, who lived in the town of Jerusalem. He loved God very much. God told Simeon a special secret. God promised Simeon that he would see Jesus in his own lifetime. This secret made the old man happy and excited. Simeon waited for the day when he would see the special baby.

Then one day, when Simeon was in the temple, Mary and Joseph walked in carrying baby Jesus. Right away, Simeon knew this baby was God's Son. He had waited so long to see and touch Him. How happy he was to finally see the baby Jesus.

Mary handed the baby to Simeon. He rocked Jesus in his arms. "Thank You, God, for this very special baby. And thank You for keeping Your secret promise to me," prayed Simeon.

Standing near Simeon was an old woman who lived and helped at the Temple-church. Her name was Anna. Every day Anna prayed to God.

When Anna saw Simeon holding the baby, she said, "This child is God's Son. He is the one we've been praying and waiting for! I know God has sent Him to help us. Thank You, God, for Your Son, baby Jesus."

Questions:
1. Who held baby Jesus? (Simeon)
2. Who prayed to God every day? (Anna)

Activities:
1. Simeon thanked God for letting him see Jesus. Name some things (or people) that you are thankful for. What can we thank God for? (ideas: Jesus, family, friends, toys, food, flowers, Grandma, Grandpa, love, secrets)
2. Whisper a secret in your child's ear (suggestion: "God loves you. So do I.").

Prayer:
Dear God, thank You for this story about Jesus and Simeon and Anna. And, thank You for _____, _____, _____ (mention the things listed in the activity ideas). Amen.

GIFTS TO REMEMBER
MATTHEW 2:1-11

Come, let's bow down and worship him. *Psalm 95:6*

It's fun to get and give gifts, isn't it? _____, listen while I read you a story about gift-giving.

The children sat beside the pretty Christmas tree. "Ding-dong!" rang the doorbell. When Mother opened the door, there stood Grandma and Grandpa with gifts for each child.

"Book!" shouted little Bobby when he opened his package. He climbed into Grandma's lap as she read this story.

One night long ago, a star shone brightly in the sky. "Look! The 'Jesus' star," said some Wise-men who studied about the stars. So these Wise-men followed the moving star until it came and stopped over Jesus' house. The Wise-men were filled with joy as they got on their knees in front of little Jesus. They worshipped Jesus and gave Him gifts. It was a very special night!

Grandma closed the book and said, "Maybe these were the first Christmas presents ever given. Now we give gifts at Christmas to celebrate Jesus' birthday.

Question:
Who followed a shiny star to find baby Jesus? (the Wise-men)

Activities:
1. Sing "Twinkle, twinkle shiny star . . ." to the tune of "Twinkle, Twinkle Little Star."
2. Worship means to tell and show God we love Him. We can worship Him by giving gifts to Jesus. Name gifts we might give to Jesus (ideas: our singing; gifts of money to church; obeying parents).

Prayer:
Dear Jesus, like the Wise-men, I give You gifts of _____ and _____ (from activity ideas). I worship You and love You. Amen.

THE CARPENTER'S SON
LUKE 2:39, 40

The little child began to grow up. He became stronger and wiser.

Luke 2:40

_____, have you ever moved to a new house? If you have, you remember what it feels like, don't you? You have a new house, new friends, new stores, and a new church. Many things are different when you move.

Jesus moved three times when He was very little. First, Jesus lived in the city of Bethlehem. (The Wise-men visited Him there.) Then, He moved with His parents, Mary and Joseph, down to Egypt. They moved there because an angel told Joseph to stay away from bad King Herod. After they stayed in Egypt for awhile, they moved back to Mary and Joseph's hometown of Nazareth.

Jesus lived with His family in the city of Nazareth when He was a boy. He had His birthdays there. He played with His brothers and sisters. Jesus helped His mom and dad, like you help Daddy (Mommy) and me. He helped His dad, Joseph, work in the carpenter's shop.

The Bible says that Jesus grew to be strong, just like you are growing to be strong. Every day, Jesus learned many new things. He learned to count. He learned to read. He learned to wash and clean up. He also learned about His Father, God. He learned to love God.

Questions:

1. Name three places Jesus lived as a child. (Bethlehem, Egypt, Nazareth)

2. Who grew up to know about and love His Father, God? (Jesus)

Activity:

Fill in the blanks with your name, city, and state:

"_____ lives in _____, _____."

Prayer:

Dear God, Jesus grew up to be strong. He learned many things. Most of all, He learned about You. And He learned to love You. Please help me as I grow up. I want to learn about You, too. Amen.

15

A FAMILY TRIP
LUKE 2:41, 42

Let us praise his name together. Psalm 34:3

_____, do you like to go on family trips? Jesus' parents went on a trip every year. When Jesus got to be about twelve years old, He went along with them. They always went to the same place at the same time each year. They traveled to the city of Jerusalem to go to the Feast of the Passover.

The Passover was a very special time for God's people. God had done many wonderful things for His people. He had saved them from the bad king of Egypt who was hurting them. So God told them to remember how He had helped them. They had a festival called Passover.

 All God's people took a trip to Jerusalem at this time. They would travel to Jerusalem with their family and friends in March or April. They celebrated like you and I celebrate a birthday. God gave them special instructions about how to celebrate this time of year.

Joseph and Mary and Jesus obeyed God. They went together to Jerusalem. Along the way they probably laughed and sang songs and played games just like we do when we go on trips. It was a family time, a time to obey and praise God together.

Questions:
1. Why did Joseph and Mary travel to Jerusalem each year? (to celebrate the Passover)
2. Who told them to celebrate the Passover? (God)

Activity:
It was about 60 miles from Nazareth to Jerusalem. Give an example of a place 60 miles from your home. Explain that Jesus' family had no car or bus. They had to walk or ride on a donkey, so it was a long, hard trip. Remember together the happy times of a recent family trip.

Prayer:
Dear God, Jesus and His mom and dad went together on a family trip to Jerusalem. They wanted to obey You. Please help our family to worship and obey You, also. Amen.

16

WHERE'S JESUS?
LUKE 2:41-46

Children are a gift from the Lord. *Psalm 127:3*

_____, have you ever been lost from your parents? When your parents could not find you, what did they do? They came to look for you, didn't they? That is what Mary and Joseph did when they couldn't find Jesus.

One day when Jesus' family was traveling home from the Passover trip, Mary asked, "Where's Jesus?"

"Maybe He is traveling with friends," said Joseph. "Let's go see." But Jesus was not with the others.

"Let's go back to Jerusalem. Maybe we will find Him there," said Joseph. Jesus' parents looked for Him for three long days. Finally they went to the Temple-church.

"I see Him!" said Mary. "He's sitting over there with the teachers." Jesus was teaching the Temple-church teachers what He knew about God. Jesus liked to talk about His heavenly Father, God.

Mary and Joseph were happy to find Jesus. They loved Jesus and went to look for Him when they thought He was lost.

Questions:

1. How long did Mary and Joseph look for Jesus? (three days)

2. Where did they find Jesus? (in the Temple-church talking with the teachers)

Activities:

1. Point to the city of Jerusalem (in the picture).

2. Play hide-and-seek with your child, or play a quiet game of "I See Something." Example: Say, "I see something that is red (blue, green . . .)." Then the child guesses until he(she) says what you're thinking about.

Prayer:

Dear God, Jesus' parents loved Him. They missed Him when He was gone and went to look for Him. Thank You that my parents love and care for me, too. Amen.

LET'S GET READY!
MATTHEW 3:1-6

Prepare in the desert the way for the Lord.
Isaiah 40:3

_____, let's pretend that Grandma is coming for a visit. What do we do to get ready? First, we make sure that we will be home. We make a room or bed ready for her. We look forward to talking with her and listening to her.

Do you remember the story about Zechariah and Elizabeth and their baby boy, John? God told Zechariah that John would grow up to be a special messenger for Him. John became known as John the Baptist, and he was a preacher who told people to get ready for a visit from Jesus. John the Baptist said, "Get ready for Jesus. He is coming soon. Be ready to listen to Him. Jesus is God's Son. He will help you to know God. Make room in your heart for Him."

John the Baptist lived in the desert, away from the city. He had a very different life. His clothes were made from camel's hair. He ate locusts dipped in honey. People from the city of Jerusalem came out to the desert to visit this strange preacher. They listened to John talk about Jesus. He told them to turn away from the wrong things they did. He told them to get ready, because Jesus was coming. Some people believed John. Some people did not.

It is like that now. Some people believe when we tell them about Jesus. And some people do not believe.

Questions:

1. Who told people about Jesus' visit? (John the Baptist)

2. What did John tell people to do? (Get ready to listen to Jesus. Make room for Him in their hearts.)

Activity:

Eat a cracker spread with honey.

Prayer:

Dear God, thank You for sending Jesus to earth. Thank You also that John the Baptist helped to get people ready to believe Jesus. I want to make room in my heart for Jesus. Amen.

A VOICE FROM HEAVEN
MATTHEW 3:13-17; JOHN 1:29-34

A voice came from heaven and said: "You are my Son and I love you. I am very pleased with you." *Mark 1:11*

_____, who did John the Baptist talk about? Yes, he talked about Jesus Christ, the Messiah. He said, "Be ready, because one of these days Jesus is going to come and talk with you."

While John was meeting with the people, he looked up to see Jesus walking toward him. "Look," said John. "Here comes the one I am telling you about. I know that He is the right one. Here is what happened that made me sure that He is God's Son.

"The other day Jesus came and asked me to baptize Him in the river. I didn't want to at first, but Jesus told me that it was good to do. So I baptized Him. After He came up out of the water, a wonderful thing happened. A dove came and rested on Jesus. A voice from heaven said, 'This is my Son. I love Him very much. I am happy with everything He thinks, says, and does.'

"I know that God is telling me that this man is the person I have been waiting for. He is that man I have been talking about. He is the Son of God."

What God says will always come true. Even if we have to wait. These people waited for Jesus, the Messiah, for many years. But God said that this special man would come. And He did.

Questions:
1. Who baptized Jesus? (John the Baptist)
2. What happened when Jesus came out of the water? (A dove rested on Jesus and a voice from heaven said, "This is my Son.")

Activities:
1. Draw a picture of a dove-bird.
2. Be a messenger for God. Tell one of your friends about Jesus.

Prayer:
Dear God, You said that Jesus is Your Son. I know You love Jesus, and I know You love me. Amen.

TWO BROTHERS MEET JESUS
JOHN 1:35-45

He said to Simon, "We have found the Messiah." *John 1:41*

_____, do you have a brother? Do you know someone who does? Having a brother is special. Many times brothers want to share with each other. Andrew and his brother were fishermen. Andrew wanted to share with his brother. Here is what he did.

One day Andrew met Jesus. He thought Jesus was wonderful. Andrew said, "I want to go get my brother, Simon. I want him to meet Jesus, too." So he ran to find Simon and brought him back to Jesus.

"Look," Andrew said to Simon. "We have found the Messiah." (Many people had been watching for the Messiah to come for a long time. Andrew knew Jesus was the Messiah they'd been waiting for.)

Jesus smiled at Simon. "I know that your father's name is John," He said. "Your name is Simon, but we are going to call you Peter."

Andrew invited his brother Simon to come meet Jesus. Then Jesus became the friend of both brothers. Andrew and Peter followed Jesus and became His special helpers.

Jesus needed more special helpers. So the next day Jesus met another man. His name was Philip. "Follow me," Jesus said to Philip.

Now Philip had a friend named Nathanael. Philip was so excited about meeting Jesus that he wanted to tell his friend. Philip said to his friend, "Remember we heard that a special man is coming. We have found Him. His name is Jesus." And Philip took his friend to meet Jesus. Philip and Nathanael also became Jesus' special helpers.

You and I can invite someone to meet Jesus, too. We can share the good news about Jesus with our family and friends.

Questions:
1. Who was Andrew's brother? (Simon)
2. What did Jesus call Simon? (Peter)

Activities:
1. Pretend to invite someone to church with you (idea: Hold play phone to ear; knock on some wood like you are knocking on a door).
2. Make an invitation with paper and crayons. Give the invitation to a friend. Invite your friend to come to church or your house.

Prayer:
Dear Jesus, _____ is my friend's name. Help me when I tell him(her) about You. Amen.

DON'T LEAVE WITHOUT ME
JOHN 1:35-42

Then Andrew took Simon to Jesus. *John 1:42*

"Petey is my best friend, Mom. I wanta ask him to come to Vacation Bible School with me. Is that OK?" asked Angie.

"I think that's a good idea," answered Mom. "Why don't you go over to his house right now and ask him? Tell him that we'll leave tomorrow morning at 9:00. He can ride with us."

The next morning Angie hurried to get dressed. She was so excited. Today was Vacation Bible School and Petey was going with her. After breakfast, Angie ran to Petey's. She knocked softly but nobody came to the door. Angie walked to the back door and knocked louder, but still no one came. "Where is Petey?" thought Angie.

Just then, Petey popped his head out the back window. "Hi, Angie!" Petey said sleepily. "Whata ya want?"

"Today's Vacation Bible School day," said Angie quietly. "I thought you were comin' with me."

"Oh, I forgot!" said Petey. "I'll hurry and get ready! Don't leave without me!"

Petey and Angie were friends. They liked to do things together. And Angie wanted to share about Jesus with Petey.

_____, we can share with our friends just like Angie did.

Questions:

1. Who is Angie's best friend? (Petey)
2. Where did Angie ask Petey to go? (Vacation Bible School)

Activities:

1. Play with your friend today.
2. Pray for your friend today.

Prayer:

Dear God, You are my friend. I pray that You will become _____'s friend, too. Amen. (Fill in the blank with your friend's name.)

22

JESUS AT A PARTY
JOHN 2:1-11

You believed in Christ (Jesus). *Ephesians 1:13*

_____, do you like to go to parties? It's fun to go to a party, isn't it?

One day Jesus went to a party with His new friends. Jesus' mother was at the party, too. This party was for a man and a woman who had just been married. Lots of people came. The party lasted a long time. All the people were talking, eating, and having a good time when they saw that they had a problem. They had run out of drink.

When Jesus' mother, Mary, saw the problem, she had an idea. Mary said to the party workers, "Jesus can help. Do whatever He tells you."

So the workers listened to Jesus. He said, "See these six water jars. Fill them up to the top with water." The workers did what Jesus said. How surprised they were when they then started to pour the water from the jars! It was not water anymore! Then they tasted it. It was the best-ever drink! Jesus made it that way. This was Jesus' first miracle.

After this, Jesus did many miracles. He did very special things that no one else could do. Only Jesus could change the plain water into the best-ever drink.

Jesus' new friends, Simon, Andrew, Nathanael, and Philip believed in Him when they saw Him do this miracle. Jesus had power to do special things. You and I can believe in Him, also.

Questions:

1. Where did Jesus, his mother, and his friends go? (to a wedding party)

2. What did Jesus do? (changed water into the best-ever drink)

Activities:

1. Have a pretend "tea" party or pretend wedding.

2. Count to six. (There were six water jars.)

Prayer:

Dear Jesus, when You did Your first miracle Your new friends believed in You. I believe in You, too. Amen.

DO YOU BELIEVE, NICODEMUS?
JOHN 3:1-21

God gave his Son so that whoever believes in him
may have eternal life. *John 3:16*

_____, a long time ago there was a man named Nicodemus. He was an important leader in the church. One night Nicodemus came to Jesus. He wanted to talk to Jesus alone. There were things about Jesus' teachings that Nicodemus didn't understand, and he wanted to ask Jesus about them.

"Teacher, You must be sent from God," Nicodemus said. "No one can do the wonderful, special things that You do unless God is helping him."

"Yes, Nicodemus. You are right," said Jesus. "I come from God. He is my Father. The way to know God is to believe me. If you believe in me and obey my commands, you will live with God forever. This is God's way. Do you understand?"

_____, just because Nicodemus was a leader in the church does not mean he understood all about God. Jesus came to help all people know about God. He came to help all people love God. Each person has to decide if he will believe Jesus and His words. Will you?

Questions:
    1. What was the church leader's name? (Nicodemus)
    2. How can we know and love God? (by believing His Son, Jesus)
Activities:
    1. Say Ni-co-de-mus.
    2. Name things that a teacher does (ideas: tells you about new things; tells you how to do something; cares about you).
Prayer:
    Dear God, You sent Jesus, Your Son. I believe in Jesus, and I believe in You. Help me as I learn about You and try to understand Your Word, the Bible. Amen.

WHO'S THIRSTY?
JOHN 4:1-30

The water I give will give him eternal life. *John 4:14*

_____, do you ever feel tired? Sometimes you need to rest, don't you. I do, too. And so did Jesus.

Jesus had been on a long trip. It was about dinner time when He came to a town called Sychar in Samaria. "I'm tired," He thought. So He sat down beside a well (a hole in the ground where water comes up).

While He was sitting by the well, a woman came. She had a water jar with her. "Would you please give me a drink?" asked Jesus.

The woman turned to Jesus. She was surprised! "You want me to give You a drink? Why?" she asked. "I thought you Jews did not like us Samaritans."

"You do not know who I am, do you? If you knew who I am, you would ask me for a drink," He said.

The woman did not understand. "What is He saying?" she thought.

"I want to give you something even better than this water," Jesus said. "I want to help you know God. I want to make your heart happy. I want to give your heart a 'happy' drink. Believe me. I am telling you the truth."

The woman was so excited about what Jesus said that she left her water jar by the well and ran to tell her friends. Then the woman's friends came to see Jesus, too.

Questions:
1. Where did Jesus rest when He was tired? (by a well in Samaria)
2. Who came by? (a woman)

Activities:
1. Get a drink of water.
2. Talk about how it feels to be very thirsty and how it helps to take a drink of water.

Prayer:
Dear Jesus, I can get a drink of water when my throat is thirsty. And I can get a drink from God when my heart is thirsty. Amen.

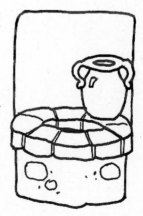

25

JESUS HELPS A LITTLE BOY
JOHN 4:43-54

The Lord is not slow in doing what he promised. *2 Peter 3:9*

Samaria is the place where Jesus talked to the woman at the well. Many people in Samaria wanted to talk to Jesus, so He stayed there for two days. Then Jesus traveled to Galilee.

While Jesus was in Galilee, one of the king's important men came to see Him. "Jesus," called the man. "Please come to my house. My little boy is very sick. Please come and make him well. We need You."

Jesus looked at the sad father. He cared about him and his sick boy. "OK," said Jesus. "But you go on home now. I don't need to come to your house. Your son is going to be alright."

The man believed Jesus' words. He turned around and started the long walk back to his house.

While he was walking along the road, people from his house ran up to him. "Guess what?" they said. "Your son is not sick anymore."

The man was so excited. "When did he get better?" the father asked.

"Yesterday at one o'clock," they said.

Then the father remembered. That was the same time that Jesus had said, "You go home now. Your son will be alright."

_____, Jesus promised to make the little boy well and he did. Jesus can do very special and wonderful things. These special things are called miracles.

Questions:
1. What did the father ask Jesus? (Please come to my house. My son is sick.)
2. Did Jesus go to the house? (no)
3. Did Jesus make the boy well? (yes)

Activity:
1. Draw a picture of the boy before and after Jesus made him well.

Prayer:
Dear Jesus, You said that You would make the little boy well and You did. I know that You always do what You say. Amen.

A SPECIAL POOL
JOHN 5:1-9

And immediately the man was well. John 5:9

_____, do you like to swim in the pool in the summer? It feels good on a hot day, doesn't it?

Let me tell you a Bible story about a very special pool. The pool was in the city of Jerusalem. It was near the Temple-church. It was different than a swimming pool. Many sick people sat around this special pool. The pool was a spring, and when it bubbled up, the sick people tried to go into the water. They thought that if they could touch the water that they might get well.

One day Jesus walked by this pool. He saw a man lying beside the water. This man had been very sick for 38 years. That is a long time. Jesus cared about the sad man. He said, "Do you want to be well?"

"Yes," said the man. "But I don't have anyone to help me get into the pool."

Right away, Jesus said, "OK, then stand up. Pick up your blanket and walk."

The surprised and happy man obeyed Jesus. As soon as he stood up, he could walk! For 38 years the man had been sick, but now he was well!

Jesus cared about this sick man. He cares about you, too.

Questions:
1. Who stayed around the special pool? (sick people)
2. How long had the man in the story been sick? (38 years)
3. Who made the man well? (Jesus)

Activities:
1. Pretend the bathtub is a special pool. Watch your child as he plays in the water.
2. Send a card or pictures to someone you know who is sick.

Prayer:
Dear Jesus, You loved and cared for the sad sick man. I know You love and care for me, too. Amen.

THE BEST DOCTOR
MARK 1:29-31

And she was healed. Jesus healed many. Mark 1:31, 34

_____, have you ever had a high fever? You were very sick, weren't you?

One day, Jesus met a woman who was very sick with a high fever. She did not feel well at all. She was in bed. But Jesus cared about her. He went to her house.

Jesus, come over here," said her friends. "Simon's mother-in-law is very sick. She has a fever. Would you please help her?"

So Jesus went over and stood by her bed. He took her hand and helped her get up. When He touched her, the fever went away. And she was well.

"Jesus, I will get You and the others something to eat now," she said, and she got up and served them.

When Jesus made Simon's mother-in-law well, she wanted to thank Him by fixing Him dinner. That night, all the people of the town brought their sick friends to Jesus, and He healed them. Jesus cared about all the hurting people.

Jesus is the best doctor.

Questions:

1. Where did Jesus go? (to the sick lady's house)

2. Who was the lady Jesus touched and made well? (Simon's mother-in-law)

Activities:

1. Pretend to make food to eat and serve it to your mom and/or your dad.

2. Talk about fevers and temperatures (normal temperature: 98.5; high temperature: 103-105).

Prayer:

Dear Jesus, You cared that Simon's mother-in-law was sick. I know that You care about me and my family, too. You are the best doctor. Thank You. Amen.

EARLY MORNINGS WITH JESUS
MARK 1:32-35

Early the next morning, Jesus woke and went to pray.
Mark 1:35

Jesus was very busy. Always people crowded around Him. He made the blind to see and the crippled to walk. He talked to sad parents. He was the children's teacher. He was a friend, helper, and teacher to His special followers, the apostles. He cared about all the sick people and made them well.

At night, after a long working day without a nap, Jesus must have been very tired. Maybe He wanted to sleep late the next morning, to get some extra rest. Some mornings, He may have done that. But many mornings Jesus woke up early, even before the birds began to sing. He woke up early to pray. What do you think Jesus talked to His Father, God, about?

Maybe He talked about His long days with the crowds pushing around Him. Maybe He told God about the blind and crippled people. Maybe He asked God to help the sad parents and to love the little children. Maybe He asked God to give Him power to make the people well.

_____, we do not know for sure what Jesus prayed about. But we know that He thought it was very important to pray to His Father. If it is important for Jesus, it is important for you and me.

Questions:
1. What did Jesus do in early morning? (pray)
2. Is it important to pray? (yes)

Activities:
1. Name the things that you did today (or yesterday).
2. Name some things to tell God about in your prayer.

Prayer:
Dear God, yesterday I _____.
Today I _____. Please help me as I try to make You happy with the things I do. Thank You. Amen.

GOD CARES ABOUT BIRDS AND YOU
MATTHEW 6:25-34

So don't worry about tomorrow.
Matthew 6:34

God makes the birds that fly in the sky. God also makes the beautiful flowers in your garden. And God made you. _____, God always takes care of everything that He makes.

While Jesus sat on the grassy hillside, He talked about the birds and flowers. He said, "Don't worry about having lots of new clothes. And don't worry about having enough food to eat. God always takes care of the birds and the flowers. And He will take care of you, too. Remember, God knows that you need to have food and clothes, and He will help you."

God cares about the baby ducks on the pond in your back yard. He cares about the robin you see outside your bedroom window. He knows about the flower seeds that you planted into the dirt in the Spring. But *you* are more important and more special to God than the birds or the flowers.

Don't worry! God loves you. He will take care of you today and tomorrow.

Questions:
1. Who made the birds to fly up in the sky and the flowers to grow from the earth? (God)
2. Does God know that you need food and clothes and a place to live? (yes)
3. Who is more special and important to God than the birds and flowers? (ME!)

Activities:
1. Name some of the different kinds of birds or flowers that God has made (ideas: robins, sparrows, bluebirds, eagles, daisies, roses, buttercups).
2. Find pictures of birds or flowers from a magazine. Cut them out and paste them on a page.

Prayer:
Dear God, thank You for making the birds that fly in the sky and the flowers that grow in my flower garden. Thank You for taking care of them. Thank You for making me. Thank You for taking care of me. Amen.

HELPING A FRIEND
MARK 2:1-12

Share with God's people who need help. *Romans 12:13*

_____, what would it be like if you could not throw a ball? Or feed yourself? Or run outside and play? How would you go to church or school or grandma's house? Mom, Dad, or a friend would have to carry you, wouldn't they?

Once there was a man who could not walk or move his arms. He could not go where he wanted to go. But this man had four very good friends. They said to him, "Jesus is in town. We want to take you to see Him." So they carried the man out the door and down the road. Soon they came to the house where Jesus was teaching. But there were so many people they could not see Jesus. There were people crowded in the doorways and in the yard. There was just no room for the man in the house where Jesus was.

"What can we do?" his friends wondered. But then they had an idea! "Let's make a hole in the roof of this house. Then we'll help our friend down through the hole. We'll put him right in front of Jesus." It was a good idea. And that's just what they did!

Jesus looked down at the man that lay on the floor in front of Him. Then He looked up at the man's four good friends on the roof. "You brought your friend to see me. You knew I would help him move again. You had a lot of faith and that makes me happy." Then Jesus said to the man on the floor in front of him, "Stand up. You can walk home now." Right away the man stood up. And he walked out with all the people watching.

His four friends were very happy to see him well. They thanked God.

Questions:
1. Who took the man who could not move to see Jesus? (four of his friends)
2. Did Jesus help the man to move again? (yes)

Activity:
Name ways you can help a friend when he needs help (ideas: listen to him; send a card; give him a ride to church; tell him Jesus loves him; pray for him).

Prayer:
Dear God, these four men loved and helped their friend. Help me to help my friends, too. Amen.

ERICA AND KELLY
MARK 2:13-17

To God every person is the same. *Acts 10:34*

Erica whispered to Kelly. "You know that new girl, Ruthie? Doesn't she dress funny? I don't like her. She wears an ugly coat. And she can't even run. She walks to preschool because her mom doesn't have a car. Let's not ask her to my birthday party."

"But," said Kelly, "she looks like she's all alone. Maybe she'd like to come to your house for the party."

"Naw, I don't think so. She's different! She doesn't even talk very well," said Erica. "But let's ask Brittany! She's pretty! And I think she has a new bicycle. Maybe she'll let us try to ride it."

Mother stood at the door of Erica's bedroom. She heard what Erica said. It made her very sad. It sounded like Erica thought just like some of the people in the Bible. They thought that some people were more important than others. This made Jesus sad, too. But God loves *all* people. He listens and cares about *all* people.

_____, God wants *all* people to know and love His Son, Jesus.

Questions:

1. What did Erica whisper to Kelly? (I don't like Ruthie; she's different.)

2. Why did Erica want to invite Brittany to the party? (She's pretty. Maybe she would let them ride her new bicycle.)

3 Who was sad when she heard what Erica said about Ruthie? (Erica's mom)

Activities:

1. Choose your own happy or good ending to the story of Erica and Kelly.

2. Talk about how you would feel if you were Ruthie.

Prayer:

Dear God, You think all people are important. You love all people the same. Help me to treat *all* people with kindness and love. Amen.

LEVI'S DINNER PARTY
MARK 2:13-17

Never think that some people are more important than others.

James 2:1

One day Jesus took a walk by the lake. Lots of people crowded around Him. But Jesus saw a man sitting in his office working. His name was Levi. Jesus walked up to Levi and said, "Come and go with me." So Levi stood, left his office and followed Jesus.

That night Jesus went to a dinner party at Levi's house. Many of Levi's friends were there. The church leaders, called Pharisees, did not like Levi's friends. The Pharisees thought that Levi's friends were not good enough to be eating with Jesus. "Why does Jesus spend time with these wild people? They don't do and say the right things," said the Pharisees. But Jesus heard what the Pharisees were saying.

"I came to help people who need help. I did not come to help those people who already think they are too good. People who are sick need to go to a doctor. And people who are well do not need to go to the doctor. I came to help the people who know they need help from God."

_____, Jesus said these words so the Pharisees would understand. He wanted them to know why He talked and ate with all kinds of people.

Questions:
1. To whom did Jesus say, "Come and go with me"? (Levi)
2. Whom did Jesus come to earth to help? (those who need and want His help)

Activities:
1. Have a pretend dinner party.
2. List ways we need Jesus' help (ideas: To obey Mom and Dad; to have "courage" when it's dark; to share; to know how to talk to God; to understand Bible stories).

Prayer:
Dear Jesus, I know I need Your help, and I know You came to help me. Please help me today when I _____. Thank You. Amen.

DOING GOOD
MARK 3:1-6

Which is it right to do on the Sabbath day: to do good, or to do evil?

Luke 6:9

A man with a crippled hand was in the synagogue one day. His hand did not work like your hand, _____.
He could not pick up books or food or toys with his hand. When Jesus saw the man, He wanted to make his hand better.

But it was the Sabbath day. The Jewish people had a rule. They could not do any "work" on the Sabbath day. They even said a person could not do good things on this special day. Jesus wanted to do a good thing. He wanted to make the man's hand well.

Jesus tried to talk to the people. He wanted them to see that it was always right to help someone, even on the Sabbath day. But they did not care about the crippled man. They only cared about the rule. This made Jesus very sad.

"Let me see your hand," Jesus said to the crippled man. Then Jesus made his hand well. Jesus cared more about the man and his problem than He did about the rule. This made the Jewish leaders very mad. They wanted Jesus to follow *all* the rules, even when the rules did not help people.

Questions:
1. Who made the man's hand well? (Jesus)
2. Why was Jesus sad? (Because the Jewish leaders were mad that Jesus would help the man. They cared more about the rules than they did about the man whose hand did not work.)

Activity:
Try to play or eat with one hand (hold the other behind you). Try to turn pages of a book and hold it at the same time.

Prayer:
Dear Jesus, You cared about the man whose hand did not work right. The people were mad. But You still cared anyway. I know You care about me, too. Amen.

JESUS' FRIENDS
LUKE 6:12-16; MARK 3:13-19

Jesus chose 12 men and called them apostles. *Mark 3:14*

Friends are very special and important people, aren't they, _____? Jesus thought friends were important, too. He had twelve close friends.

One night Jesus walked by himself up a tall mountain. He wanted to be alone so He could talk to God. He prayed to His Father, God, all night long. Maybe He prayed to God about His friends.

The next morning, Jesus called His twelve friends to a meeting. "I'm glad we are all together," He said. "I have chosen you twelve to be my special helper-friends. I am going to call you 'apostles.'" I want you to go with me on my trips. You, too, will preach and help people."

Jesus loved and cared about His special friends. They spent a lot of time together. They helped Jesus tell others about God.

Four of Jesus' special friends were named Peter, John, Andrew, and Matthew. Do you have any friends with these names?

Questions:

1. What did Jesus do when He went up on the mountain? (He prayed to God.)

2. What name did Jesus give to His twelve special helper-friends? (apostles)

Activities:

1. Name three of Jesus' friends/apostles. (The names of Jesus' apostles not mentioned above were: James, Philip, Bartholomew, Thomas, James, Thaddaeus, Simon, and Judas Iscariot.)

2. Name three of your friends.

Prayer:

Dear Jesus, thank You that You had twelve special friends that spent lots of time with You. Thank You, too, for my special friends _____, _____ and _____. Amen. (Fill in the blanks with the names you mentioned in the activity.)

FAITH
MATTHEW 8:5-13

Faith means being sure of the things we hope for.
Hebrews 11:1

_____, Jesus is the best doctor ever. He makes people well. He helps our doctors to help us.

One day a leader of the army said to Jesus, "I have a man who works for me. He is very sick. He is at home in bed. He cannot move his arms or legs. Would You please make him well?"

"Yes, I will come to your house and make him well," Jesus answered.

"But I am not good enough for You to come to my house," said the army leader. "You can just make my worker well from right here. I know that You can do that!"

Jesus was surprised and happy to hear the army leader say these words. "This man really believes in me," said Jesus to the people watching. I've never seen anyone with this much faith." Then He looked at the man. "Go on home, now," He said. "I have made your worker well. He is feeling better already."

Jesus was happy with the army leader. Many of the army leaders did not love or believe God, but this man did. Sometimes the leaders did not care about the people who worked for them. But this man was different. He cared about his worker. He asked Jesus to help.

We, too, can ask Jesus to help other people. We can pray to God. Jesus wants to help our friends.

Questions:

1. Whose worker was very sick? (an army leader)

2. Did Jesus make the army leader's worker well? (yes)

Activities:

1. Name people that Mom and/or Dad work with.

2. Name friends you play with.

Prayer:

Dear Jesus, would You please help _____ and _____. Thank You. Amen. (Fill in the blanks with answers from the activity.)

THE TINY SEED
MATTHEW 13:1-9, 18-23

That seed is like the person who hears the teaching (of God) and understands it. *Matthew 13:23*

_____, do you like to listen to a story? Yes, I know that you do. Jesus liked to tell stories. He told His followers lots of stories. Many of Jesus' stories are called "parables." Parables are short stories that teach a lesson.

One day Jesus told a parable about a little seed. Have you ever seen the tiny seed inside an apple? Jesus talked about a seed just like that. He said that if you plant that little apple seed in good dirt, that it will grow up to be a strong tree. But if you try to plant that little seed on the driveway or in the rocks, it cannot grow up.

Jesus said that little seed is like the little boy or girl who hears about God. When the little boy or girl believes the words about God then he can grow up to be strong in God's love. The little boy or girl can grow to love and know God.

Jesus told His followers many stories. We can read these stories in the Bible.

Questions:

1. Who liked to tell stories? (Jesus)

2. What do we call the stories of Jesus? (parables)

3. What does the little apple seed grow up to be if you plant it in good dirt? (a strong tree)

4. Who is the little seed like? (a little boy or girl who hears about God)

Activities:

1. Eat an apple and keep the little seed that is inside.

2. Look at the strong tree outside your window. Talk about how it grew from a little seed.

Prayer:

Dear God, I hear about You. I believe Your words. Thank You for helping me to grow strong in loving You. Amen.

JESUS STOPS A STORM
MATTHEW 8:18-27; LUKE 8:22-25

He made the storm be still. Psalm 107:29

_____, have you ever taken a boat ride?

One day Jesus and His special friends decided to take a boat ride. They rowed back and forth across the lake.

Soon it began to rain. "There's a storm coming!" they cried. The wind blew hard. The waves hit the sides of the boat. The boat started to fill up with water. Jesus' friends were afraid. But Jesus was taking a nap. He was very tired.

"What shall we do?" thought Jesus' friends. They shook Jesus to wake Him up. "Teacher, we're in a bad storm. Do You care about us? We might drown if the boat sinks."

Jesus opened His eyes and stood up. He said, "Quiet, storm! Wind, be still!" And right away the wind stopped blowing and the water was quiet. He did something no one else could do. His friends were learning more about Jesus every day.

"Even weather and nature obey Him," they said.

Questions:

1. What kind of a ride did Jesus and His friends take? (They took a boat ride.)

2. What happened while they were on the boat? (A storm came and Jesus' friends became afraid.)

3. Who stopped the storm? (Jesus)

Activities:

1. Make believe that you and one of your friends are rowing together in a boat.

2. Draw a picture of Jesus in the boat telling the wind to be quiet. Show the happy faces of Jesus' friends.

Prayer:

Dear Jesus, You and Your Father, God made the water in the lake and the wind. All the weather and nature obey You. You are very strong. Amen.

WHO TOUCHED ME?
MARK 5:25-34

No one can do the miracles you do, unless God is with him.

John 3:2

Everyone wanted to see Jesus. Lots of people followed Him day after day. He healed and helped many people. He was very busy. Sometimes He did not even have time to eat.

One day Jesus was walking along the road. People were bumping into Him. It was very crowded. A sick woman was in the crowd of people. She had been sick for twelve years. No doctors could help her. She spent all her money on medicine, but nothing helped her get well.

The woman had heard about Jesus. "If I can just get close to Him," she thought. "I won't bother Him. But if I can only touch His clothes, I know I can get well." She reached out her hand to touch His coat. Right away she felt better. She knew her sickness was gone.

But just then Jesus turned around. He stopped walking. "Who touched my coat?" He said.

"How can You ask that question?" the people said. "Lots of people are bumping into You."

Then the woman answered, "Jesus, I'm the one who touched You. And now my sickness is gone."

Jesus said, "Dear woman, I'm glad you believe in me. Now you are well. Go on home and be happy."

Questions:

1. Who touched Jesus? (a woman who'd been sick for twelve years)

2. Did Jesus make her well? (yes)

Activities:

1. Count to 12. (That is how many years the woman had been sick.)

2. Count how old you are. Fill in this blanks with your name and age: _____ is _____ years old.

Prayer:

Dear Jesus, You were glad when the woman believed in You. You are happy when I believe in You, too. Amen.

HAPPY PARENTS
MARK 5:21-24, 35-43

Don't be afraid; only believe. Mark 5:36

An important leader of the church came to see Jesus one day. This man was also a daddy. And his heart was sad. "My little girl is sick," he said. "She is so sick that she might die. Please come to our house. You can make her well, I know."

So Jesus started to walk with the daddy to his house. On the way some men ran up to them. "Sir, your little girl has died. So Jesus doesn't need to come anymore."

But Jesus turned to the daddy and said, "Don't worry! Don't be afraid! Just believe." And He kept right on walking. When He got to the house, they could hear all the people crying loudly. There was a lot of noise.

Jesus said, "Mom and Dad, you come inside with us. The rest of you people stay here." Then Jesus walked into the girl's room. He took her hand and said, "Little girl, get up now." Her mother and father watched in surprise as their daughter stood up and walked around. They were very happy parents. Jesus did what no one else could do.

_____, we can believe whatever Jesus says. Jesus always does what He says He will do. When we are afraid, we can trust Him to help us.

Questions:
1. Who came to Jesus? (a church leader, a daddy)
2. What did he ask Jesus? (My little girl is very sick. Please come to our house and make her well.)
3. What happened to the little girl when Jesus came to the house? (She got up and walked around.)

Activity:
Draw a happy picture of the Mom, Dad, and little girl after Jesus came to their house.

Prayer:
Dear Jesus, I believe that You always know how to help me. Amen.

THE BIG PICNIC
MATTHEW 14:14-21; JOHN 6:3-13

He cares for you. *I Peter 5:7*

Do you like to go on picnics, _____? I know that you do! Listen while I tell you about a very big picnic!

A great crowd of people had followed Jesus all day. As the sky became dark, stomachs began to growl. The people were hungry. There were so many people that the apostles wondered how to feed them all. Andrew told Jesus that a small boy wanted to share his lunch of five buns and two fish.

So Jesus told all 5,000 men with their families to sit on the ground and get ready for a big picnic. Jesus first thanked God, His Father, for the food. Then the apostles passed lunch out to the men, women, and children. After everyone had eaten all that they wanted, the apostles had twelve baskets full of leftover food.

 Jesus loved and cared for the many hungry people. He did something no one else could do with the five buns of bread and two fish. He took this small lunch that the little boy had and made it become enough food for more than 5,000 people.

Jesus loves and cares about you, too. He will do special things for you.

Questions:

1. What did Jesus do for the big crowd that no one else could do? (He fed them with five loaves of bread and two fish.)

2. Who did Jesus thank for the food? (God, His Father)

Activities:

1. Sing "Jesus Loves Me" with your child.

2. Eat a small bun or roll for lunch. (Talk about what a special thing it was for Jesus to take such a small amount of food and feed over 5,000 people with it.)

Prayer:

Dear Jesus, thank You for loving the crowds of people, and thank You for loving me, also. Amen.

WHO IS MOST IMPORTANT?
MARK 9:33-35

Do not be interested only in your own life,
but be interested in the lives of others. *Philippians 2:4*

Jesus and His helper-friends went on a long walk to the city of Capernaum. Jesus' friends talked with each other as they walked. One helper said, "I was thinking. Which one of us is more important? Does Jesus love you more? Or does He love me more?"

One said, "I can sing better than you. I must be more important."

"But I can talk better than any of you," said another. "I think I'm more help to Jesus." The helpers did not talk to Jesus about this. They only talked with one another.

When they came to the city, Jesus asked, "What were you talking about on our walk here?" But no one answered Jesus! Maybe they felt shy about what they had been talking about.

Then Jesus sat down with the twelve men. He said, "Don't always try to be the first one or the most important one. Choose to be a helper to me and to each other." Jesus told them that it was not important to decide who was better than any one else.

_____, we all are important to Jesus. He cares about all of us. And He wants us to care about each other, also.

Questions:

1. What did Jesus' helper-friends talk about while they were walking to the city of Capernaum? (who was the best or most important)

2. Who said, "Don't always try to be the first one or the most important one"? (Jesus)

Activity

Name all people in your family. (Explain to your child that Jesus and His helper-friends were like a big family. They ate together. They took trips together. They spent lots of time together.)

Prayer:

Dear Jesus, I want to be a helper to You and other people. Help me not to think that I always have to be the first one. Thank You. Amen.

LITTLE LOST LAMB
MATTHEW 18:10-14

The Lord is my Shepherd. *Psalm 23:1*

A long time ago there was a shepherd who had 100 sheep. He took good care of the sheep. He walked with his sheep every day. He knew the big ones and the small ones, the fat ones and the skinny ones. He knew the white ones and the black ones.

One day as he walked with the sheep, he saw that one of his little lambs was missing. "Where is this little lamb?" he thought. "I must go look for it." So the shepherd left the 99 sheep safe at the farm. Then he went out to find the little lost lamb.

The shepherd looked everywhere for his lost sheep. He looked by the lake. He walked down the path to the forest. He climbed up the hill and walked around the big rocks.

Suddenly he heard a noise. "What is that I hear?" he said.

"Ba-a-a! Ba-a-a!"

"Maybe it's my little lost sheep!" said the shepherd. He ran toward the noise. Just then he saw the little lamb caught between two big rocks. Carefully the shepherd reached down and picked up the scared, shaking lamb. "I am so happy I have found my little lamb. He is not lost anymore," said the shepherd.

_____, Jesus told this story to His friends and followers. He said the kind shepherd is like God. He does not want any little child to be lost without Him. He wants each little child to believe in Jesus. He loves and cares about every boy and girl just like the shepherd cares about every little lamb.

Questions:
1. How many sheep did the shepherd have? (100)
2. What did the shepherd do when he realized one of his sheep was missing? (He looked for the sheep until he found it.)
3. Who is like the kind shepherd? (God)

Activities:
1. Count to 100 (or count to 10 and say that 100 is a lot more than that).
2. Draw a picture of the little lost lamb.

Prayer:
Dear God, thank You for caring about each little child just like the kind shepherd cared for each little lamb. Amen.

BORN BLIND
JOHN 9:1-39

Yes, Lord, I believe! *John 9:38*

_____, close your eyes. Can you see anything? Everything is dark, isn't it? Now, open your eyes. Aren't you glad that you can see?

One day Jesus was taking a walk with His friends. They walked past a man who could not see. Even when he was a baby he could not see. "This man was born blind so that God can make him see again," said Jesus. "This will show how powerful my Father is."

Then He leaned over and put mud on the man's eyes. "Now go and wash off in the Siloam pool."

The man did what Jesus told him to do. "I can see," he shouted. "I can see."

But the church leaders who did not like Jesus tried to make trouble for the man, his parents, and for Jesus. "Why can you see now?" they asked the man. "How did it happen?"

"The man named Jesus did it," he said.

"Well, we think you are telling a lie," the church leaders said. "We don't believe that you are the same man who was blind. Maybe you just look like him."

Then the man's parents became afraid of these people. They said, "Yes, this is our son. Yes, he was born blind. But don't blame us. We don't know who this Jesus is."

Then Jesus himself came back up to the man and asked, "Do *you* believe in me?"

"Oh, yes," the man answered. Then he bowed and worshipped Jesus.

Questions:
1. Who did Jesus and His friends see while they were taking a walk? (a man who had been born blind)
2. What did Jesus do? (He made the man to see.)

Activity:
Choose several familiar small toys. Now tell your child to close his eyes and feel the toys with his fingers. Tell him to try to guess what they are without opening his eyes.

Prayer:
Dear Jesus, the man believed in You even when the other people did not. I believe in You even when my friends do not. Amen.

HELPING
LUKE 10:25-37

Share with God's people who need help. *Romans 12:13*

_____, who is one of the neighbors on your street? Yes, he(she) lives in your neighborhood. One day a man asked Jesus, "Who is my neighbor?" Then Jesus told this story.

A man was walking down the road. Some bad men came up and hit him. They hurt him. They tore his clothes. They took all his money. They left him alone in the street.

Then a church leader walked down the same road. He saw the man, but he walked on by. He did not stop to help. Another man who worked at the Temple-church walked down the road. He went over to look at the hurt man on the ground. But he did not help him.

Then a man from a different town came down the road. He saw the hurt man. He saw his torn clothes, his cuts and broken bones. He cared about him. He put medicine on his "owies." He lifted him up on his donkey and took him to the town motel. He paid for the motel room and gave him some food. He showed that he cared about this hurt man.

When Jesus finished the story, He turned and asked, "Which of these three men was a real neighbor to the hurt man?"

"The one who helped him was the real neighbor," answered the men.

"Then go and help others just like he did," said Jesus.

Question:

Who in the story was the "real neighbor" and helped the man who had been hurt? (the man who was from a different town)

Activities:

1. Name ways we can be a good neighbor (ideas: give food or clothes to a food shelf or mission; send a card to a sick person).

2. Plan to do one of the things you named above.

Prayer:

Dear God, help me to care about and help my neighbor. Amen.

SISTERS MARY AND MARTHA
LUKE 10:38-42

How I love your teachings! *Psalm 119:97*

Jesus went to visit Mary, Martha, and Lazarus. Martha and Mary were sisters and Lazarus was their brother. They were happy when Jesus came to visit them. Mary thought Jesus was the best teacher ever. She loved listening to His stories. Mary sat on the floor in front of Jesus. She was quiet while He talked about His Father, God.

Her sister Martha hurried around the house. She baked bread for dinner. She cleaned up the room where Jesus would sleep. She made the soup for the meal. She even swept the floor around Mary and Jesus while they talked. She was getting tired from working so hard and fast. Then she started to get mad because she was doing all the work by herself. So she stopped sweeping and said to Jesus:

"Lord, look at my sister. Is she lazy or something? Don't You care that she is making me do all the work. Make her get up and help me!"

Jesus looked up at Martha with the broom still in her hand.

"Martha, listen to me. You are worried about too many things. You don't have to do all these things to get me to love you. I love you anyway. I love Mary, too. And Mary is doing the most important thing. She is listening to God's words. Let the soup cook. Come visit with me."

_____, Jesus wants us to listen to God's words (the Bible) and spend time with Him (in prayer).

Questions:

1. Who was busy working? (Martha)
2. What did Jesus want Martha to do? (sit and listen to God's words)

Activities:

1. Read the verse at the top of the page. Say it together.
2. Sweep the floor.

Prayer:

Dear God, Jesus says that it's important to listen to Your words. Help me to remember that. Amen.

HOW TO PRAY
LUKE 11:1-4; MATTHEW 6:9-13

"Lord, please teach us how to pray, too." *Luke 11:1*

_____, prayer is talking to God. Jesus prayed to God. Sometimes He prayed together with His friends. And other times He was alone when He prayed to His Father, God.

One time, after Jesus prayed alone, a helper-friend said, "Lord, please teach us how to pray."

So Jesus said, "When you pray, say:

'Dear Father, You are very wonderful and good. May everything that You want come true. Please help us to have the food we need for each day. Forgive and forget the bad things we do. We will forgive and forget the bad and wrong things people do to us. Please help us to do the right things (like obeying Mom and Dad, saying thank you and being kind). You are great and stronger than any one. Amen."

It is very important to pray to God. Jesus prayed. He knew how important it was to talk to His Father.

Jesus taught His followers how to pray, and He teaches us how to pray. We can learn to pray to God by following Jesus' example in the Bible.

Questions:

1. What is "talking to God" called? (prayer)

2. Did Jesus ever pray with his friends? (yes)

3. Did Jesus ever pray to God by himself? (yes)

Activity:

Name things we can pray about (ideas: We can tell God that He is good (praise Him); We can ask for what we need—food, clothes, a place to live; We can tell God we're sorry when we do wrong; We can thank God.).

Prayer:

Dear Father, You are so good to us. Thank You for giving us food and clothes and a place to live. Help me to obey You tomorrow/today. I love You. Amen.

49

HELPING THOSE WHO CAN'T HELP YOU
LUKE 14:12-14

Then you will be blessed, because they cannot pay you back.
Luke 14:14

_____, do you like to visit your friend's house?
It is nice when your friend invites you to come over, isn't it?

One day a man invited Jesus to come over to his house for dinner.
While Jesus was there, He asked, "Did you invite only your neighbors
and friends who have lots of money? They are sure to ask you to their
house next time. Then you will get a free meal. Is that why you asked
all these people?

"I have a better idea," said Jesus. "The next time you have a dinner
party, ask the people who don't have lots of money. Ask the blind or
hurt or crippled people to come. Ask people who can't pay you back.
They can't ask you to their house. If you do this, you will be helping
the people who need it. You will be helping the people who can't help
you back."

It is alright to share with your friends. It is good to invite them to
your house. But Jesus said that it is also good to ask the people who
cannot ask or help you back. This is a special kind of sharing. It will
make you very happy to share this way.

Questions:

1. What did Jesus tell the man who had invited Him to dinner?
(Next time, invite people who can't invite you to their home.)

2. Does Jesus want us to do things for people who can't do things
for us? (yes)

Activity:

Name a way you could help someone
who could not help you back (ideas: go
to a nursing home; give money or
clothes to homeless people; visit someone in the hospital; ask someone to your
home; give money or send a "care"
package to a missionary).

Prayer:

Dear Jesus, I want to help someone
who can't help me back. Please help my
family and me to do that. Amen.

WILL AARON SHARE?
LUKE 12:13-21

A generous person will be blessed. *Proverbs 22:9*

"No," yelled Aaron. "You can't listen to my records."
Danny cried. He was visiting at Aaron's house. But Aaron did not want to share his new records and record player with him. So Danny walked away into Aaron's bedroom.

"No! No!" shouted Aaron. "Don't go into my room. It's *my* room." Danny was sad. His friend, Aaron, was being selfish. But Danny left Aaron's room and went into the kitchen. He reached up and took an apple from the bowl on the table. He started to take a bite when Aaron yelled again, "No, Danny! That's *my* apple. Don't eat *my* apple."

That's when Danny yelled back. "You're mean, Aaron! I'm going home! I don't want to play with you anymore." Danny put on his coat and headed for the front door.

Aaron saw his friend, Danny, go out the door. "I guess I was being selfish," he thought. "Now Danny is going home."

He walked to the door.

"Danny," he called. "I'm sorry. I'll share my room and records with you. Please come back."

Danny turned around. He ran to hug Aaron. He was glad that Aaron changed his mind.

_____, God is glad when we share. He is also happy when we say we're sorry when we have done selfish things.

Questions:
1. Why was Danny sad? (His friend, Aaron, was being selfish.)
2. Did Aaron say he was sorry? (yes)

Activities:
1. Play a record on your record player (if available).
2. Share an apple with your child.

Prayer:
Dear God, I am sorry when I don't share. Please help me to share when I play with my friends. Amen.

WELCOME HOME
LUKE 15:11-24

Being sorry in the way God wants makes a person change
his heart and life. *2 Corinthians 7:10*

_____, Jesus told a special story about a father and
his boy. One day the boy came to his father. "Dad," he said, "I want my
money, and I want it now. I am going to move away from home." So
the father gave his son the money that was his. And the boy left.

He went to a faraway place. When he got there he bought lots of
new things. He went to big parties. He spent all his money. Then he
had no money left for food. And he had no bed to sleep in. The boy
was hungry, so he got a job. It was the only job he could find. It was
not a nice job. He fed the pigs on a man's farm. He ate the pig's
sloppy food because he was so hungry. It was a dirty, icky job.

One day the boy sat down in the middle of the pigpen. He was
dirty, hungry, sad, and alone. "I know I was wrong to leave my father's house, but what should I do now?" The boy thought for a while.
Then he said, "I will go back and tell my dad that I'm sorry I left. I'll
ask Dad to let me work for him." So the boy stood up and left the pigpen. He walked all the way home.

Before the boy even got to the house, his father saw him on the
road. He ran to meet him. He hugged him. The boy said, "I was
wrong, Dad. I'm sorry."

His dad said, "You're back. I'm so glad. Let's have a great big wel-
come-home party."

Jesus said that God is like the dad. We are like the boy. Sometimes
we do things that take us away from God. But when we tell God we
are sorry for the wrong things we do, then He welcomes us back.

Questions:
   1. Who took his money and left his father's house? (the boy)
   2. Was the dad happy when his boy came home again? (yes)
Activity:
   Make a sound like the pigs.
Prayer:
   Dear God, Jesus said You are happy (just like the father was) when
a boy or girl comes and prays to You. I am sorry when I do wrong
things (like disobeying or hitting my friend). Thank You for loving
me. Amen.

ONE LOST DIME
LUKE 15:8-10

There is joy when one sinner changes his heart. *Luke 15:10*

Once there was a woman who had ten shiny dimes. One day when she counted her dimes, she only had nine. One dime was gone.

"Where could it be?" she thought.

So she got a light and looked all over her house. She cleaned every room, looking under the beds and in the closets. At last she found it! She was very happy. She called her friends to tell them her wonderful news.

_____, Jesus told this story to His friends. Jesus told many stories. He told this story because He wanted the people to know how much God loved each one of them.

God cares about *every* person.

Ten people are together in a room. But only nine of the ten people believe in God. God wants the one person who does not believe God to change his mind. When that one person changes his mind to believe in God, God is very happy.

He is happy just like the lady who found her one lost dime.

Questions:
1. How many dimes did the woman have? (ten)
2. What happened to one of the dimes? (She lost it.)
3. Was she happy when she found it? (yes)
4. Is God happy when one person changes his mind to believe in Him? (yes)

Activities:
1. Give your child a dime.
2. Trace the dime ten times on a piece of paper. Color nine of the circles red and one green.

Prayer:
Dear God, You are happy every time someone believes in You. I believe in You. Amen.

54

WHERE'S LAZARUS?
JOHN 11:1-44

I am the resurrection and the life. *John 11:25*

_____, do you have a very good friend? What is your friend's name?

Jesus had three very good friends. There were two sisters named Mary and Martha, and a brother named Lazarus. Jesus liked to visit them in their home. They lived in the town of Bethany. Where does your friend live?

One day Jesus' friend Lazarus became sick and died. When Jesus got to Bethany, He saw Lazarus' sisters, Mary and Martha, and all the crying friends.

Jesus was so sad that He cried, too. "Where did you bury my friend, Lazarus?" He asked.

"Come here and we will show You," they said.

"Move that rock away from Lazarus' grave," said Jesus. Then He prayed to His Father, God.

"Lazarus, come out now!" said Jesus in a loud voice. And guess what? Lazarus came out. Jesus made Lazarus come back to life. Jesus did something no one else could do.

Questions:

1. What were the names of Jesus' good friends? (Mary, Martha, and Lazarus)

2. Who became sick and died? (Lazarus)

3. Who prayed to God? (Jesus)

4. What happened to Lazarus? (Jesus said for him to come out of the tomb, and he did.)

Activity:

Make a sad face. Make a glad face.

Prayer:

Dear Jesus, You are the only one who could make Lazarus come back alive. You are very great. Amen.

HAPPY OR SAD TEARS?
JOHN 11:1-44

Lord, you know everything. My cries are not hidden from you.
Psalm 38:9

Little Randy skipped into the dining room. He stopped when he saw his mother sitting in a chair. She was crying. He walked slowly over to the chair and laid his soft head on mother's lap. "Happy tears, Mommy?" he asked.

She hugged her young son's chubby neck. "No, Randy, sad tears. Mommy has sad tears this morning."

"Sorry," said little Randy. He loved his mother and shared her sadness.

_____, do you remember when Mary and Martha cried sad tears because their brother, Lazarus, had died? Jesus loved them and shared their sadness. Sometimes we have happy tears. That happens when we're so excited or happy that we feel like crying. Sometimes we have sad tears. That happens when we lose someone or something that we care about. Randy's mother was sad because her friend had died that morning.

Jesus shares our sadness and always, whether we have sad or happy tears, Jesus loves us.

Questions:

1. Who said, "Happy tears, Mommy?" (a little boy named Randy)

2. Who cried sad tears when Lazarus died? (Lazarus' sisters, Mary and Martha, and Jesus)

3. Does Jesus care when we have tears? (yes)

Activities:

1. Hug your child.

2. Draw a picture for someone you know who has sad tears. Send it to them.

Prayer:

Dear God, You know everything. You see when I have happy or sad tears. Thank You for loving me always. Amen.

THE THANK-YOU STORY
LUKE 17:11-19

Give thanks whatever happens. 1 Thessalonians 5:18

_____, what is the best thing to say when some-one does something nice for you? You're right. You should say "thank you." Listen to this story about nine men who forgot and one man who remembered to say thank you.

When Jesus was walking along the road one day ten men called to Him. These ten men were different. They were lepers and very sick. Leprosy was a disease that was so "catchy" that even to touch someone meant that you might get it. They were so sick they could not even live with their families. "Jesus! Master! Make us well!" the lepers cried.

Jesus felt sorry for the sick men and He made them well. They were so happy. Now they could go live with their family and friends again. They all ran their own way.

But suddenly one man turned and ran back to Jesus. He fell on his knees in front of Jesus saying, "Thank You! Thank You for making me well."

Jesus was very pleased with this one man. But He wondered about the others. Didn't He also heal them? But they did not take the time to come back and thank Jesus. Only one man remembered to thank Jesus for healing him.

We, too, can remember to be thankful. This pleases Jesus.

Questions:
1. What did the ten lepers ask Jesus to do? (make them well)
2. Who healed the ten sick men? (Jesus)
3. How many came back to thank Jesus? (only one)

Activity:
Jesus wants us to be thankful, also. Tomorrow (or other later time) I will put a star on this page every time you remember to say "thank you."

PARENTS: Remember to put the book in a convenient spot. (If you have gold sticker stars that would be nice; but if not, simply draw your own star with a red pencil or crayon.)

Prayer:
Dear Jesus, thank You for this story in the Bible about saying "thank you." Please help me tomorrow to remember to say "thank you" when someone does something nice for me. Amen.

JESUS LOVES THE CHILDREN
MARK 10:13-16

Let the little children come to me. *Mark 10:14*

_____, do you like to be hugged? It feels good when I hug you and tell you that I love you, doesn't it? It is nice to know when someone loves you.

Jesus loved *all* little children. A long time ago moms and dads would walk long ways just to bring their boys and girls to Jesus. They were so excited to have Jesus hug their children. Jesus would let the children sit on His lap while He talked to them.

But Jesus' helper-friends said, "Go away and stop bothering Jesus. Can't you see that He is very busy?" It made the moms and dads very sad.

Jesus heard what His helpers said. "It's OK," He said. "Bring the little boys and girls to me. They are very special. The children love and believe me. The big people should come love and believe me like the children do."

Then Jesus took the children in His arms. He hugged them. He asked His Father to make the little children happy. Jesus knows that children are special.

Jesus loves all little boys and girls. He loved the children who lived a long time ago. And He loves the children who live right now. He loves you!

Questions:
1. Who loves all children? (Jesus)
2. Who said for the parents to keep the children away? (Jesus' helper-friends)
3. Who hugged the children? (Jesus)

Activities:
1. Give your child a hug. Ask your child to give you a hug.
2. Today (tomorrow) tell one of your friends or a brother or sister about Jesus. Tell him(her) that Jesus loves all children and that Jesus loves him(her).

Prayer:
Dear Jesus, thank You for loving me and letting me come to You. Amen.

GOOD FRIENDS TALK
MATTHEW 20:17-19; MARK 10:32-34; LUKE 18:31-34

He taught that the Son of Man must be killed
and then rise from death after three days. *Mark 8:31*

_____, what is your good friend's name? Do you like to do things together? Do you share with each other? Do you tell each other things?

Jesus and His good friends liked to do things together, too. They shared food and work and play. They walked together a lot. Jesus told his twelve special friends many things. He talked to them about what was going to happen to Him.

"We are going to the city of Jerusalem," He said. "Some of the church leaders there do not like me. They do not believe I am really God's Son. They want to kill me. When we get to the city they are going to hurt me and laugh at me. I am going to die. *But* I am going to come back alive after three days."

Jesus cared about His special friends. He did not want them to be surprised when these sad things happened to Him. So even before they got to the city, He told them what would happen. He loved them and cared about their feelings.

Questions:
1. What did Jesus and His friends do together? (ate, played, worked, talked)
2. Who said that He would die and then come back alive after three days? (Jesus)

Activities:
1. Name some things that you and your friends do together.
2. Count to twelve (for the twelve special friends).

Prayer:
Dear Jesus, I know that You cared about Your twelve special friends. You told them about what was going to happen to You. You cared about their feelings. You care about my feelings, too. Thank You. Amen.

SAMMY NEEDS HELP
MARK 10:46-52

I wait for the Lord to help me. *Psalm 130:5*

"I'm five years old now. I'm so big. I don't need Mom's help anymore," Sammy thought. "Maybe I'll clean my room. No, I could do that when I was four. I can put my toys away. No, I could do that when I was three. I know! I'll vacuum the carpet." He opened the closet door and looked up at the vacuum cleaner. It looked big and heavy.

"I can do it!" he said to himself. He grunted and groaned as he pulled it out. When he turned it on, it made a whirling noise. "Uh oh! I can't make it go where I want it to go," he thought. "It's too hard! Oh, no!" CRASH! BANG! Sammy stared at the broken lamp on the floor. Tears came into his eyes. Mother came running from the kitchen.

"What happened?" asked Mom.

"I wanted to show you how big I am," said Sammy. "I wanted to show you that I don't need your help anymore." Tears rolled down his cheeks. "I'm sorry, Mom."

Mom looked at her sad "big" boy. She bent down to hug him. "Oh, Sammy, sometimes you *do* need my help. You can't do everything by yourself, right?" Sammy nodded his head up and down.

_____, sometimes you and I think we don't need God's help. But we do. You can't do everything by yourself. And I can't do everything by myself.

Questions:

1. How old was Sammy? (five years old)

2. Did he need his mom's help? (yes)

Activities:

1. Name times when we need God's help (ideas: to obey; to tell the truth; to share; to be kind to others; to not be afraid in the dark).

2. Put your books on the shelf.

Prayer:

Dear God, sometimes I think I don't need help. Then something happens that shows me I do. Help me to wait for Your help. Amen.

WHO CLIMBED A TREE?
LUKE 19:2-10

"Whoever loves God must also love his brother." *1 John 4:21*

_____, what does it feel like to be shorter than other people? What happens when you are with grown-ups and can't see over their heads? Someday you'll grow to be taller. But once there was a man who didn't grow to be very tall. His name was Zacchaeus. He was short, but he was very important in the town. He had lots of money.

One day Jesus came to Zacchaeus' town. "I want to see Jesus," he said. "But a lot of people are in my way. What should I do?" Zacchaeus thought about it. Then he had an idea. "I'll climb a tree and sit in the top branches. Then I'll get to see Jesus." So that is what he did.

When Jesus walked down the road, He stopped under the tree Zacchaeus had climbed. He looked up and saw the short man sitting in the top branches. "Zacchaeus," called Jesus. "Come down here, because I want to stay at your house tonight." This surprised Zacchaeus, but he quickly obeyed. He was glad that Jesus was coming to his house.

But the people were grouchy about it. "Why is Jesus going to Zacchaeus' house?" they asked. "He is a man who cheats and sins. Nobody likes him."

But Zacchaeus changed his heart and life when he met Jesus. "I want to give my money to help the poor people. And I will give back the money I took from the townspeople. I will even give them back more than I took." Zacchaeus made up his mind to follow Jesus. Sharing his money was just one way he showed that he loved Jesus.

Questions:

1. How did Zacchaeus see Jesus? (He climbed a tree.)

2. Where did Jesus stay? (at Zacchaeus' house)

Activities:

1. Sing the song, "Zacchaeus Was a Wee Little Man."

2. Supervise your child while he(she) climbs a tree.

Prayer:

Dear Jesus, I'm going to follow You, just like Zacchaeus. Amen.

THE PONY RIDE
LUKE 19:28-34; MATTHEW 21:8, 9

"Rejoice. Shout for joy. Your King is coming.
He is on the colt." *Zechariah 9:9*

_____, point to the
pony in the picture. Would you like to take a
ride on a pony some time?

One day Jesus took a ride on a colt. (A
colt is a baby horse or a baby donkey, often
called a pony.) Listen to a story about when
Jesus took a pony ride.

"Walk into town, get a pony and
bring him to me." Jesus said to His
friends. "Tell the pony's owners that I
need him."

Jesus' friends did just what He
asked them to do. Then His friends
took off their coats and put them over the back of the pony. It
was like a saddle. Jesus climbed up on the pony's back. Many
people cut branches off trees and laid them down on the ground.
It was like a nice carpet for Jesus to ride on. The people walked
beside Jesus and the pony. They all had a great time.

"How wonderful Jesus is!" shouted the people. "He is King.
He makes blind people see. He loves children. He is the special
man God promised to send."

Grown-ups and children sang praises to God. You and I can sing
happy songs about Jesus, too.

Questions:
1. What did Jesus ask His friends to do? (go into town and bring a
pony to Him)
2. Who took a pony ride? (Jesus)

Activities:
1. Pretend to ride a pony (on someone's knees or on a chair).
2. Go on a walk with your child. Collect small tree branches.

Prayer:
Dear God, I want to tell how happy I am that Jesus came. I praise
You just like the people in this story did. Amen.

LOVING
MATTHEW 22:23-40; MARK 12:28-34

Love the Lord your God with all your heart, soul and strength.
Deuteronomy 6:5
Love your neighbor as you love yourself. *Leviticus 19:18*

_____, what do you think is the most important rule in the Bible? What is the greatest thing God tells us to do?

A long time ago the church leaders asked Jesus these same questions. "Teacher, what is the most important thing that God tells us to do?" asked one of the church leaders. Again, they tried to trick Jesus with their hard questions. But He was very wise.

Jesus answered, "The greatest and best thing to do is to love God. Love Him with your whole heart. Love Him with all your thinking. Love Him in everything you do." The leaders were surprised with Jesus' answer.

Then Jesus said, "And the number two important rule is to love and care about other people as much as you love and care about yourself."

"What you say is true," said one of the leaders. Then no one ever asked Jesus a trick question again.

It is important to share. It is important to say thank you. It is important to always tell the truth and not lie. But the most important thing is to love God; and love others like you love yourself. When you love God, you will want to share, say thank you, and tell the truth. You show that you love others and yourself when you do these things.

Questions:
1. What is the most important rule? (to love God)
2. What is the number two important rule? (to love others like you love yourself)

Activity:
Hug me. Hug yourself. Now reach up and pretend to hug God.

Prayer:
Dear God, I want to love You and others and myself. Please help me. Amen.

GIVING
MARK 12:41-44; LUKE 21:1-4

Each one should give what he has decided in his heart to give.
2 Corinthians 9:7

_____, one day Jesus and His friends were in the Temple-church. Jesus sat down beside the Temple money box. People walked by and put in their money gifts to God. The rich people came by. They put lots of money into the box.

Then a poor woman came to the Temple-church. This woman lived all alone. She didn't have much money. So why did she stop beside the money box?

Jesus and His friends watched her put two small coins into the box. It did not even add up to one penny. But it was all she had. Jesus turned to His friends and said, "This poor lady gave only two coins. But she gave more than all the rich people. The rich people gave money that they didn't need or even care about."

This lady gave a love gift to God. When she put her last two coins into the box, she believed that God would take care of her. She wanted to show God that she loved Him.

We, too, can give a love gift to God. We can give some of our money (or our time) in helping and sharing with others.

Questions:

1. Where were Jesus and his friends? (in the Temple-church by the money box)

2. How much money did the poor woman put into the money box? (two coins, less than one penny)

3. Why did she give? (because she loved God)

Activity:

Save a few coins (pennies, nickels, dimes) to give to church or a charity. Keep them in a safe place (money box) until time to give.

Prayer:

Dear God, I give my money and time to You because I love You. Amen.

JUDAS

MATTHEW 26:14-16; MARK 14:10, 11; LUKE 22:1-6

Judas was the one who gave Jesus to his enemies.
Matthew 27:3

_____, how many special helper-friends did Jesus have? Yes, He had twelve special helper-friends. Jesus and His twelve helpers spent a lot of time together. They were together when Jesus healed many people. Jesus taught them how to pray. Jesus taught them about His Father, God.

But one of Jesus' helpers just pretended to love and follow Jesus. This man's name was Judas Iscariot. He was not a true helper or a true friend of Jesus.

One day Judas made a very bad decision. He went to see the jealous church leaders. (The church leaders did not like Jesus. They were looking for a way to hurt Him.)

 Judas said to the leaders, "I will give Jesus to you. But I want you to pay me money for doing this. How much money will you give me for tricking Jesus?"

The church leaders gave Judas thirty silver coins. Then Judas went back to be with Jesus and the eleven other helpers. He acted like he loved Jesus, but he did not. He planned and waited for the best time to give Jesus to the jealous church leaders. Judas was not a true friend or follower of Jesus.

Questions:
1. What was the helper's name who did not really love Jesus? (Judas Iscariot)
2. Who did Judas talk to about Jesus? (the jealous church leaders)
3. Did Judas make a good (wise) decision? (no)

Activity:
Count to thirty. Judas got thirty coins from the church leaders.

Prayer:
Dear Jesus, Judas was with You every day. But he did not really love or follow You. I really want to follow You. Please help me. Amen.

KRISTEN SHOWS LOVE
JOHN 13:34, 35

Love each other. *John 13:34*

_____, Jesus told His helpers something special while they were eating dinner together. Let me tell you what He said to them.

Jesus said, "Love each other. Love each other the same way I have loved you. People will know that you are my friends and followers if you love each other."

Kristen's teacher at church had read these words from the Bible. "How can I show my friend, Nicki, that I am Jesus' friend and follower?" she thought.

The next day Kristen and Nicki were playing hide-and-seek outside. It was Nicki's turn to hide. So Kristen closed her eyes and counted to ten. When she opened her eyes and looked she could not find Nicki anywhere. She looked in the back yard behind the shed. She looked in the front yard by the bush. She looked under the porch. She even looked up in the tree.

Then Kristen heard a soft cry. What was that sound? She ran to see. It was coming from Nicki! Nicki's arm was caught in a fence. She was cut and bleeding.

"Oh, Nicki, you're hurt," said Kristen. "I'll run to get help." So Kristen ran up to the house.

"Mom," she yelled through the door, "Nicki needs help. Come quickly!" So Mom followed Kristen to see Nicki. Together they untangled Nicki's arm from the fence. Then they cleaned and bandaged the cut. Kristen hugged Nicki. Kristen was happy to show love to Nicki when her friend couldn't help herself.

Questions:
1. What did Jesus tell His helpers at dinner? (love each other)
2. Who showed love to Nicki? (Kristen)

Activity:
Plan to play hide-and-seek.

Prayer:
Dear Jesus, please help me to show love to my friends. Amen.

JESUS WASHES HIS FRIENDS' FEET
JOHN 13:1-20

"I did this as an example for you.
So you should do as I have done for you." *John 13:15*

Jesus was a great leader and teacher. His friends loved and followed Him. He did special things that no one else could do. These special things were called miracles. Jesus helped many people with His miracles. Jesus made people well. He took a boy's lunch of two fishes and three buns and made lots of food for the hungry people. He walked on the water. His Father, God, gave Him "power" to do these special things.

Jesus could have said, "Now, listen here. I am very great. No one is like me. You are my followers. So, you better do whatever I say. I will just sit here, and you get my food and drink. Bring me my clothes. And don't forget to wash my feet." But Jesus did not act like this. He always treated His friends with kindness.

One day Jesus put a towel around His waist, got a bowl or water, and began to wash His friends' feet. This was not a real "fun" job. His friends' feet were very dirty from walking on the dirt roads in sandals. But Jesus said, "I do this as an example to you. I treat people with kindness. I forgive them when they hurt me. And I want all of you to do the same thing."

_____, you and I can learn to treat other people with kindness and forgiveness like Jesus did. We are showing others about Jesus when we do like Jesus would do.

Questions:
1. Who made people well, fed hungry people, and walked on water? (Jesus)
2. How do your feet look when you walk outside in your sandals or bare feet? (they are dirty)
3. Who washed His friends' feet? (Jesus)

Activities:
1. Wash your child's feet. Let your child wash your feet.
2. Count Jesus' friends in the picture.

Prayer:
Dear Jesus, I want to treat my friends and family with kindness. I want to forgive them when they hurt me. I want to be like You. Please help me. Amen.

THE LORD'S SUPPER
MATTHEW 26:26-30; MARK 14:22-25; LUKE 22:15-20

Do this to remember me. Luke 22:19

_____, have you ever heard of the Lord's Supper? Maybe you have heard of it at church. Maybe you have not. Listen while I tell you what the Bible says about the Lord's Supper.

Jesus and His special friends were eating together. They were all at the table when Jesus picked up a loaf of bread. He prayed to thank His Father, God, for the bread. He tore it into pieces and each man ate some. Then Jesus said, "You are eating this bread so you will remember that my body was hurt and I died for you."

Then Jesus took a cup of juice. "This cup of juice will help you remember that I bled for you when I died on the cross."

Jesus had not died on the cross yet. But He was trying to help His friends understand. In a few days Jesus would die. He would die so that no one would ever again have to kill a lamb to be forgiven.

Many years before, God told His people to kill a lamb when they did bad things. This was the way that they asked God to forgive them. But now Jesus was going to die for all people. He was like a lamb. This was God's new way.

When we believe in Jesus, we become a friend of God and He forgives us.

Questions:

1. Who ate at the first Lord's Supper? (Jesus and His twelve special friends)

2. What was going to help Jesus' friends remember that Jesus died on the cross? (the bread and cup of juice)

Activity:

Take an unsliced loaf of bread or a roll and tear off pieces to eat. Talk about the first Lord's Supper.

Prayer:

Dear Jesus, I remember that Your body was hurt and that You bled when You died on the cross for me. Thank You. Amen.

THE HELPER
JOHN 14:15—16:33

I (Jesus) will send you the Helper from the Father. *John 15:26*

_____, do you know what an orphan is? An orphan is a child whose mom and dad have died.

One day Jesus was talking to His helpers about what was going to happen to Him. He said, "I will not leave you like orphans. It is true that I am going to die. But I promise to come back again. And then I will go to be with God my Father in heaven. I am not going to leave you without help. I have asked God to send you a Helper. His name is the Holy Spirit. He will be with you always. He will help you to know and tell the truth. He will help to teach you all the things I have said about sharing, loving, praying, being kind and knowing God.

"I know that you will be sad when I am gone. We have had such a good time together. But the Helper, the Holy Spirit, will come to you. He will tell you special words from me.

"Some days you might have a hard time. People might make fun of you because you love me. But be brave! The Holy Spirit will help you."

Jesus said all these words to His special friends. He says them to you and me, too. The Helper Holy Spirit is for all of us who believe in Jesus.

Questions:
   1. What is an orphan? (a child whose parents have died)
   2. Did Jesus leave His friends to be like orphans? (No, He left them a Helper.)
   3. Who was going to be their Helper? (the Holy Spirit)
   4. How does the Holy Spirit help? (helps us to know and tell the truth, helps us to be brave, helps us to know the words Jesus said, helps us pray to God)

Activities:
   1. Name ways an orphan might feel (ideas: sad, alone, scared).
   2. Plan a trip to an orphanage. Take some food or clothing for the children there.

Prayer:
   Dear Father God, thank You for sending me the Helper Holy Spirit. Holy Spirit, thank You for helping me. Amen.

JESUS' FAVORITE PLACE
MATTHEW 26:36-46; MARK 14:32; LUKE 22:39-46

Jesus was full of pain; he prayed even more. Luke 22:44

_____, do you have a favorite place to go? Maybe your favorite place is the park. Maybe it is the ball field. Maybe you have a favorite room in your house.

Jesus had a favorite place. He went there lots of times. Sometimes He took His friends with Him. Jesus' favorite place was a garden called Geth-se-ma-ne. It was on a hill. He went there to pray. The night they ate the Lord's Supper together, Jesus went with His friends to the Garden of Gethsemane.

Jesus told His friends to sit and wait for Him while He prayed. Then He walked over to a spot by himself. He knelt down to pray. He was so sad as He thought about how He was going to die.

"My Father," prayed Jesus, "I want to do what You want. But I really do not want to be hurt and die on the cross. If You want me to, though, I will do it."

Then an angel came to help Jesus. Jesus' heart was very heavy and sad. He prayed even more. Jesus prayed at the hardest and saddest time of His life. He told God just how He felt.

We can talk to God when we are sad, too.

Questions:
1. Where did Jesus go to pray? (to the Garden of Gethsemane)
2. Who went with Him? (His friends)
3. Did Jesus tell God how He felt about dying? (yes)

Activity:
Name some things that make you sad.

Prayer:
Dear Jesus, I know You were sad when You thought about dying. But thank You for doing what God Your Father wanted. Thank You for dying for me. Amen.

72

GRABBED IN THE GARDEN
LUKE 22:47-53

Christ had no sin. *2 Corinthians 5:21*

_____, do you remember the man who just pretended to love Jesus? His name was Judas Iscariot. The jealous church leaders paid him money to turn against Jesus.

One night, Judas took them to the garden of Gethsemane to get Jesus. He said, "Watch me. The man I kiss is Jesus. Take Him away. Arrest Him." So he walked up to Jesus and said, "Hello, Teacher!" Then Judas kissed Jesus.

Jesus did not run away. But the men grabbed Him. They had sticks and swords. They treated Jesus like He was a bad man. But Jesus never did anything bad in His whole life.

Peter saw what was happening. He did not like it. Peter pulled out his sword. Slash! He cut off an ear of the servant of one of the jealous church leaders. But Jesus leaned over and touched the man's ear. Right away his ear was healed.

Then a very sad thing happened. Jesus' special friends ran away and left Him alone with the jealous church leaders.

Questions:

1. Who came to Jesus in the garden and kissed Him but did not love Him? (Judas)

2. What did Peter do with his sword? (cut off the ear of one of the men)

3. Who healed the man's ear? (Jesus)

4. Who arrested Jesus? (the jealous church leaders)

Activity:

Draw a picture of the knife-like sword that Peter used to cut off the man's ear.

Prayer:

Dear Jesus, it must have hurt You very much when Judas just pretended to love You. It must have hurt You when Your friends ran away, too. Help me to always act like I love You. Amen.

MATT'S FAVORITE PLACE
LUKE 22:39, 40; MARK 14:50

I love the Lord because he listens to my prayers for help.
Psalm 116:1

Matt had a favorite place. He liked to climb up the little hill in his back yard. On the hill was a big tree. Whenever he wanted to think or "read" or talk to God, he went to his favorite spot under the big tree.

One day last week Matt ran to his "spot" on the hill. He went there all alone. He was sad. And he was mad. His friend Eric had promised to come over and play soccer with him. But Eric went to Johnny's house instead of coming to play with Matt. Eric did not keep his promise to Matt. This made Matt mad. He sat under the big tree and pouted.

But then Matt remembered about Jesus and His favorite place. "Jesus prayed when He was in his favorite place by the trees," he thought. "Maybe I'll pray for my friend Eric."

"Dear God, I was sad and mad when Eric didn't keep his promise to me. But I'm sorry for pouting. Please help Eric and me when we play together tomorrow. Amen."

Matt had a favorite place just like Jesus did. Jesus prayed to God when He went to His favorite place. He told God how He felt, and so did Matt.

_____, God always listens when we pray and tell Him how we feel.

Questions:
1. Where was Matt's favorite place? (under a tree on a hill)
2. What did he do at his favorite place? (He thought; he "read;" he prayed.)

Activities:
1. Name one of your favorite spots.
2. Draw a picture of your favorite spot.

Prayer:
Dear God, thank You for listening to me when I tell You how I feel. Amen.

LIES ABOUT JESUS
MARK 14:53-65; LUKE 22:66-71

They all said, "Then are you the Son of God?"
Jesus said to them, "Yes." *Luke 22:70*

_____, would you like it if someone told lies about you? No, I would not like it, either.

One night, years ago, people told many lies about Jesus. Do you think He liked it? (No.) The jealous church leaders asked Jesus lots of questions. They tried to trick Him and get Him in trouble. But they could not find a real reason to get rid of Jesus.

Finally, they gathered around Jesus and said, "Answer us! Are you the Son of God?"

And Jesus said, "Yes, I am. I am going to go back to heaven to sit beside my Father, God. Someday I will come back again."

The church leaders did not believe what Jesus said. They were angry because they thought Jesus was talking against God. So the angry leaders turned to the people who were watching. "What should we do with Jesus?" they asked.

"Kill Him!" the people answered. Then they spit in Jesus' face.

They slapped Him. They said many mean things to Jesus.

The people did not believe that Jesus was really God's Son. They told lies about Him. It was a very sad time.

Questions:

1. Who told lies about Jesus? (the jealous church leaders and some of the people)

2. Did Jesus say that He is the Son of God? (yes)

3. Did the people want to kill Jesus? (yes)

Activity:

Draw an angry face (or a sad face).

Prayer:

Dear Jesus, some people don't believe that You are God's Son. But I believe You. Amen.

75

THE THIEF
LUKE 23:39-43

Jesus said, "Today you will be with me in paradise!"
Luke 23:43

_____, *anyone* can believe Jesus and be with God for always in heaven. Boys and girls can believe Jesus. Moms and dads, grandpas and grandmas, people from television, people in jail—anyone can believe Jesus.

Here is a story about one man who decided to believe Jesus.

The same day that Jesus was nailed to a cross, two other men were beside Him on two other crosses. These men were thieves. They stole what did not belong to them. They disobeyed the laws and rules of their country. Their punishment was to die on a cross.

One of the men made fun of Jesus. But the other man said, "You should care about God! We have done bad things and we *should* be punished. But Jesus has not done anything wrong." He turned his head and said, "Jesus, please remember me. I believe You."

Then Jesus said to the man, "I tell you the truth. I know that you believe me. So you will be with God for always."

Anyone who believes in Jesus and obeys Him can be with God for always just like this thief. Jesus loves and accepts all kinds of people. He wants all people to come to Him.

Questions:

1. How many men died on a cross when Jesus died? (two other men-thieves)

2. Did they both believe Jesus? (no, only one)

3. Who can believe Jesus and live with God for always? (anyone)

Activities:

1. Add 2 + 1.

2. Draw three crosses on this page.

Prayer:

Dear Jesus, thank You that anyone can believe You and live with God always. Amen.

JESUS DIED
LUKE 23:44-46; JOHN 19:30

God made friends with us through the death of his son. *Romans 5:10*

_____, do you know what a cross looks like? It is two pieces of wood that are nailed together. They cross over each other to look like a +.

The angry, jealous leaders told men to put Jesus up on a cross. They nailed His hands and feet to the cross. It hurt Jesus. Jesus was hurting, tired, and sad.

Jesus talked to his Father, God, while He was on the cross. He said, "It is over. I'm finished. I give You my life." Jesus came to earth as a baby so that He could grow up and die for us. Now He had done what He had come to earth to do so He said, "It is finished."

It was about noon (lunch time) when the whole sky became dark. The sun was gone, yet it was the middle of the day! The darkness lasted about three hours. Then Jesus died.

Jesus died for a very special reason. He died to show us that God loves us. When people do bad (sinful) things they need to be "punished." So Jesus was "punished" for us. Jesus died for the bad things we do, like lying, cheating, stealing. All we need to do is believe Jesus and obey God's words. Then we can be with God for always.

Questions:
1. Who did the men nail to the cross? (Jesus)
2. What happened to the sky before Jesus died? (It turned dark for three hours)

Activities:
1. Hold up three fingers (the darkness lasted three hours).
2. Draw a cross on this page.

Prayer:
Dear Jesus, thank You for loving me enough to die for me so that I can be with God for always. Amen.

77

SECRET FOLLOWERS
JOHN 19:38-42; LUKE 23:50-56

Joseph was a secret follower of Jesus,
because he was afraid of the Jews. John 19:38

_____, do you remember who wanted to kill Jesus? It was some jealous and angry church leaders. But there was one church leader who did not like what had happened to Jesus. His name was Joseph. He was a "quiet" Jesus follower. He kept his love for Jesus a secret because he was afraid of what the other church leaders would say to him. But would Joseph stay a secret follower? No.

After Jesus died, Joseph asked Pilate if he could bury Jesus. So Pilate gave Jesus' body to Joseph.

Joseph wrapped Jesus' body in cloth rags. Joseph and a friend put Jesus' body into a hole in the side of a cave. They rolled a big stone in front of the hole to keep it safe.

Some of Jesus' friends watched. They were very sad. They loved Jesus so much. But now He was gone.

Jesus' friends did not remember the special promise Jesus had made to them. He would come back alive!

Questions:

1. What was the "quiet" Jesus follower's name? (Joseph)

2. What did Joseph do with Jesus' body? (wrapped His body in cloths and buried it in a cave)

3. Did Jesus' friends remember that He said he would come back alive? (no)

Activity:

Whisper a "secret" to your child (ideas: I love you. We will take a walk tomorrow. We're having chicken for dinner.).

Prayer:

Dear Jesus, I am Your follower. I don't want to keep that a secret. Help me not to be afraid of what my friends will say when I talk about You. Amen.

EASTER MORNING
MATTHEW 28:1-6

Jesus is not here. He has risen from death! *Luke 24:6*

_____, do you know what happened on that first Easter a long time ago? I will tell you the story. It is very exciting! There is no other story like this one.

The morning sun was just starting to peek over the hill. Two women walked to the place where Jesus' body was buried. As they walked they felt the ground move and shake under their feet. Then they saw an angel of God. He was shining like the sunshine. The clothes he had on were white like snow. He walked over to the place where Jesus was buried and moved away the heavy rock in front of the door. Then he sat down on the rock. When the two women saw the angel they were scared.

"Don't be afraid!" the angel said. "I know that you are looking for Jesus. But I have good news. He is not here! Because He is alive again! Come here, I'll show you."

Easter is the day Jesus came back to life. We are so happy that our friend Jesus did not stay dead. He did something no one else has ever done. God helped Him come back alive. Now, today, He lives with God in heaven.

Questions:
1. Who walked to the place where Jesus was buried? (two women)
2. Whom did they see? (an angel)
3. Was Jesus there? (no)
4. Why? (because Jesus had come back to life)

Activities:
1. Pretend like the ground is moving and shaking under your feet.
2. Name things that happened on the first Easter. (Refer to the story for details.)

Prayer:
Dear Jesus, You are not dead. You are alive! That is good! Amen.

"I SAW JESUS!"
MARK 16:9-11; JOHN 20:13-18

I know my sheep. And my sheep know me.
My sheep listen to my voice. *John 10:14, 15, 27*

_____, have you ever been really sad? Do you cry when you're sad?

Mary Magdalene was sad. Big tears rolled down her cheeks. She had come to the place where Jesus was buried, but the stone had been rolled away from the front of the cave. Jesus' body was not in the cave anymore.

As Mary was crying she looked inside the cave again. She saw two angels in bright white clothing. The angels asked Mary why she was crying.

"Someone has taken my Lord. I miss Him so much," she said.

After Mary said this, she turned around. There was a man standing beside her. "Why are you crying?" the man asked. "Are you looking for someone?" Mary thought the man was a worker in the garden.

"Did you take Jesus away?" she asked. "Please tell me where He is. I will go get Him."

Then the man said, "Mary." Right away, Mary knew that she was talking to Jesus. She was so glad to see Jesus. Mary's sad tears became happy tears.

"Go tell my other friends that I'm alive," said Jesus. "I will soon go back to live with God, our Father."

So Mary ran to tell Jesus' followers.

"I saw Jesus!" she said.

Questions:
1. Who had big tears rolling down her cheeks? (Mary Magdalene)
2. Why was Mary crying? (She thought someone had taken Jesus body.)
3. Who was the man standing beside Mary? (Jesus)
4. Where did Mary go after she saw Jesus? (to tell Jesus' other friends)

Activity:
Make a sad face. Make a glad face.

Prayer:
Dear Jesus, You loved and cared about Mary and her tears. I know that You love and care about me, too. Amen.

IS JESUS REALLY ALIVE?
JOHN 20:3-9; LUKE 24:12-32

Jesus talked to us on the road. Luke 24:32

_____, do you like to run? Do you sometimes race a friend to see who gets there first?

Peter and John raced each other. When Mary told them Jesus was gone, they ran to see. They ran down the street, over the hill, and through the garden. They ran hard. But John got to the cave first.

Peter came right behind him. He went into the cave where Jesus' body had been. Mary was right! Jesus was gone! The pieces of cloth that were wrapped around Jesus' body were now folded neatly. But where was Jesus? They did not understand what Jesus had told them before. They did not know that Jesus would come back to life.

Later that day, two of Jesus' followers took a walk. They talked about all that had happened. They talked about Jesus and the cross. They talked about Mary's words, "He is alive."

A man joined them on the walk. He listened to them talk. He told them what God said about Jesus coming back alive. The three of them ate together. Suddenly, they knew that the man with them was Jesus. And then in that same moment, Jesus was gone again. Then they ran to tell the other followers. "It's true!" they shouted. "Jesus is alive."

Peter and John and the other two Jesus followers were starting to understand that Jesus was alive again.

Questions:
1. Who raced each other to the tomb? (Peter and John)
2. Who did Jesus talk to? (two men taking a walk)

3. Is Jesus alive? (yes)

Activities:
1. Pretend to race two stuffed animals.
2. Plan a race outside in the yard if weather permits.

Prayer:
Dear Jesus, God had said You would come back to life. You did. Men and women saw You. It is true! Amen.

GOD KNOWS THE TIME
ACTS 1:6-8

The Father is the only One who has the authority
to decide dates and times. *Acts 1:7*

One day after Jesus came back to life, His friends asked Him a question. "Lord, are you going to be King now?" (It was a good question. It showed that they knew that someday Jesus *would* be the King.)

But Jesus said, "I do not know when I will come as the King of everyone and everything. Only my Father, God, knows when that time will be. We do not have to know these things right now. Before I become King, though, God wants you to go and tell all the people of the world about me. He will help you not to be afraid when you talk to people about me. For God is going to send the Holy Spirit to help you."

_____, one day Jesus will come back on earth. Then He will be King of everyone. We do not know when this will happen. We do not have to worry about it because God knows.

While we are waiting for Jesus to come back, we can sing about Him. We can pray and love Him. We can tell our friends about Jesus. We have the Holy Spirit to help us do these things while we wait for Jesus.

Questions:
1. Who asked Jesus when He was going to become King? (Jesus' friends)
2. How did Jesus answer them? (Only God knows when that time will be.)
3. Who will help us while we wait for Jesus to come back? (the Holy Spirit)

Activities:
1. Sing a song to Jesus. (Make one up if you want to.)
2. Name today's date.

Prayer:
Dear God, You know about all days and times. You always know what is going to happen. You know when Jesus will come back. You are my very smart God. Amen.

JESUS SAYS GOOD-BYE
MATTHEW 28:16-20; ACTS 1:9-11

He will come back in the same way you saw him go. *Acts 1:11*

_____, have you ever said good-bye to someone you love?

Jesus and His followers loved each other. They liked to do things together. The followers were sad that it was almost time to say good-bye. Jesus was going back to live with His Father, God.

One day Jesus told His followers to meet Him on a hill. "I will be waiting for you there," He said.

When Jesus' follower-friends saw Jesus on the hill, they worshipped and praised Him. They knew that Jesus was not just a man. He was different than anyone else.

Suddenly, something strange happened. A cloud came around Jesus

 and He went up into the sky. The followers stared at the cloud.

Then two men dressed in white clothes came and stood beside Jesus' friends. "Why are you standing here looking into the sky?" they asked. "You saw Jesus go up into heaven. Someday He will come back this same way."

This promise helped the followers when they said good-bye to Jesus. Jesus has not come back yet. But He will. It is a promise to us, also.

Questions:
1. What came around Jesus? (a cloud)
2. Where did Jesus go? (to heaven to live with God)
3. Who told Jesus' friends that someday Jesus would come back? (two men dressed in white clothes)

Activities:
1. Paste or glue pieces of cotton to the clouds in this picture.
2. Pretend that you are waving good-bye to someone you love.

Prayer:
Dear Jesus, the Bible says You will come back the same way You went to heaven. I don't know when it will be, but I believe it will happen. Amen.

THE HELPER GIVES COURAGE
ACTS 2:14-42

This Helper is the Holy Spirit. *John 14:26*

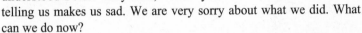

_____, do you know what the word "courage" means? Courage means to be brave, even when you feel afraid. The Holy Spirit gave Peter courage.

Peter showed he was brave when he was not afraid to tell the people the truth about Jesus. "Jesus is the special man that God promised to send to you," said Peter. "But you killed Him." Peter did not worry that the people might be mad at him for saying these words.

Peter told the people many other words, too. The people were surprised, but they understood Peter. They said, "What you are telling us makes us sad. We are very sorry about what we did. What can we do now?

"Change the way you think and believe about Jesus," said Peter. "Then you will receive the Holy Spirit to help you." About 3,000 people believed in Jesus that same day.

Peter was not afraid to tell the truth about Jesus because the Holy Spirit helped him. The Holy Spirit will help us, too. He helps us to do what we cannot do by ourselves. He helped Peter to have courage. And He will help us to have courage. God gives us the Holy Spirit to be our Helper.

Questions:
1. Who had courage and told the people the truth about Jesus? (Peter)
2. Who gives us the Holy Spirit to be our Helper? (God)

Activities:
1. Point to Peter in the picture. What is he doing?
2. Name times when you need courage (ideas: when you go to school; when it's dark; when it's time to go to sleep; when someone laughs at you).

Prayer:
Dear God, thank You for sending the Holy Spirit to be my Helper. Please help me to be brave. Thank You. Amen.

THE DR. LUKE
ACTS 1:1-5

I (Dr. Luke) wrote about the whole life of Jesus. Acts 1:2

_____, a doctor wrote the book called Acts in the Bible. His name was Dr. Luke. He wrote another book in the Bible, too. The book is named for him. It is called Luke.

Dr. Luke wrote about Jesus' life in the book of Luke. He told about when Jesus was a baby. He told how Jesus hugged and loved the children and how Jesus made the storm stop. He wrote about the people who did not believe Jesus. And he wrote about how Jesus died and then came back alive.

In the first part of the book of Acts, Luke wrote about when Jesus said good-bye to His friends. For forty days after He came back alive, Jesus talked with His friends. "Look at my hands and feet," Jesus said. "Go ahead and touch me. I am alive. I am going to say good-bye now. I am going back to heaven to be with God, my Father. But you wait here in Jerusalem. God has something special for you. Now wait and see."

These are some of the words that Dr. Luke wrote in his two books of the Bible.

Questions:
1. What was the doctor's name? (Dr. Luke)
2. What were the names of the two books that Dr. Luke wrote? (Luke and Acts)
3. What did Dr. Luke write about in his Bible book called Luke? (Jesus' life)

Activities:
1. Find the books of Luke and Acts in a Bible to show your child.
2. Make a book—fold two pieces of 8 1/2" x 11" paper and put them together to form a book. Draw inside.

Prayer:
Dear God, thank You that Dr. Luke wrote down the true stories about Jesus. Now I have a way to know about Him. Amen.

DANNY WRITES A BOOK
ACTS 1:1-5; 2:14-42

Be strong. Don't give up. *2 Chronicles 15:7*

_____, do you like to read? It's fun when we read together, isn't it? Danny liked to read, too. One day he had an idea.

"Mom," he called. "I think I'll write a book like Dr. Luke (in the Bible) did. Can I have paper and pencil, please?"

"OK, Danny," said Mom. "What will your book be about?"

"I think I'll write about 'courage.' You remember what "courage' is, don't you, Mom?" Danny didn't wait for his Mom to answer. "Courage is being brave when you feel like being afraid," he said.

Just then Danny's big brother, Sam, walked into the room. "What are you doing, little brother?" he asked.

"I'm writing a book like Dr. Luke did," said Danny.

Sam laughed. "You can't do that. You're too little. You can't draw or write very good."

Danny started to cry. "I guess I can't do it," he thought. "Maybe I can't do anything!" Then he remembered that God's Holy Spirit would help him to not be afraid to do things. "Help me to have courage," he prayed, "even when Sam makes fun of me and says I can't do it."

After he prayed, Danny turned around in his chair and started to "write" his book. He drew pictures and colored them. He wrote his name on the "courage" page of his book.

Questions:
1. Who wanted to write a book about "courage"? (Danny)
2. Who helps us to have courage? (God's Holy Spirit)

Activities:
1. Make a pretend book with your hands folded together. Open it up and say the Bible verse at the top of the page together.
2. Make a book like Danny did (ideas for supplies: 8 1/2" x 11" paper; crayons or markers; tape or staples; pictures from magazines).

Prayer:
Dear God, help me to have courage when I feel afraid. Amen.

THE MAN WHO COULD NOT WALK
ACTS 3:1-13, 16

By the power of Jesus—stand up and walk! *Acts 3:6*

_____, do you see the man in the picture sitting by the Temple-church door? He is asking people for money. He cannot work to make money for his own food. The man does not have a job because he cannot walk. His legs do not work right.

One afternoon at about 3:00, Peter and John went to the Temple-church. (That was the time of day when people stopped what they were doing to pray.) When the man saw Peter and John he asked, "Could you give me some money?"

But Peter said, "Man, I don't have any money, but I'll give you something else. By the power of Jesus—stand up and walk!" Peter took the man's hand and helped him get up. When he stood up his feet and legs were strong. He jumped and skipped and walked. He was so happy. Then he walked into the Temple-church with Peter and John. He prayed and thanked God for making his legs and feet strong and well.

The man's friends were very surprised to see him up and walking. So they ran to Peter and John. "How did this happen?" they asked.

"Well, it didn't happen just because we are good. It is Jesus who made this man walk again."

Questions:

1. What did Peter and John say to the man who couldn't walk? ("We don't have any money, but we'll give you something else instead.")

3. What did Peter and John do for the man? (God gave them the power to make the man walk.)

Activities:

1. Look at a clock or watch. Point to the 3 on the face. (This is the time the people came to pray.)

2. Draw a picture of a clock. Make it say 3:00.

Prayer:

Dear God, the happy man praised and thanked You. I thank You, too. Amen.

LISTENING TO GOD
ACTS 3:11—4:22

Should we obey you or God? Acts 4:19

Peter and John taught the people many things about Jesus. "God sent Jesus," they said. "I know that you did not understand what you were doing when you killed Jesus. But, believe what we say. Pray to God. Change the way you think and believe about Jesus."

The people listened to Peter and John teach. Some believed and prayed to God. But some of the Temple-church leaders got mad. They hated what Peter and John taught.

"Do not teach about Jesus anymore," they said. "Do not even say His name."

Peter and John asked, "But what is the right thing to do? Should we listen to you or to God? We have decided that we cannot keep quiet. We have to do what God wants us to do."

_____, has anyone ever asked you to do or say something that you knew God did not want you to do or say? Maybe a friend said, "Let's go over and pick all the apples off the neighbor's tree." But God says, "Do not take what is not yours." Who should you listen to—your friend or God?

God's Word, the Bible, tells us what to do and say to make God happy. We should always listen to God.

Questions:

1 Who didn't want Peter and John to teach about Jesus? (some of the Temple-church leaders)

2. Who asked, "Should we listen to you or should we listen to God?" (Peter and John)

Activity:

Draw a picture of an apple tree.

Prayer:

Dear God, help me to listen to You even if someone wants me to do something bad (like stealing or lying). I know that following You is always the right thing to do. Amen.

A LYING TONGUE
ACTS 5:1-11

The Lord hates a lying tongue. *Proverbs 6:16, 17*

_____, did you know that God does not like it when we lie? God still loves us when we lie, but He does not like the lying. What is a lie? It is when we do not say what really happened. It is a lie when we do not tell the truth about what we did or about how we think.

Here is a story that shows us that God does not like lies.

There once was a man and a woman named Ananias and Sapphira. They were married. They wanted to give some money to God to help the new church. So they sold some of their land. They got lots of money for the land. They kept part of the money to buy something new. That was an "alright" idea. But it was a bad idea when they decided to lie. They pretended that they gave *all* the money to God and

the new church. They tried to hide what they were doing from God. They lied. God does not like lying. Ananias and Sapphira lied to God, not just to men. Then a very sad thing happened. Ananias and Sapphira died.

God does not like lying. He knows what we think. He knows when we tell what really happened. He knows when we try to hide what happened by lying. But we cannot hide anything from God. He always loves us. And He always wants us to tell the truth.

Questions:
1. Does God like it when we lie? (no)
2. Does He still love us? (yes)
3. Who lied in this story? (Ananias and Sapphira)

Activities:
1. Play "store," buying and selling with make-believe money.
2. Take the make-believe money and divide it into two parts. One part is to give to God and one part is to keep.

Prayer:
Dear God, help me to always tell You (and other people) what really happens. I know You will help me to tell the truth. Amen.

SEVEN NEW HELPERS
ACTS 6:1-7

Help each other. *Galatians 6:2*

_____, has Mommy or Daddy ever asked you to pick up your toys or set the table or watch the baby or empty the waste basket? Do you ever feel like it's too much work for you? Sometimes you need help, don't you? When a job is too hard or too much work, we may need help from other people.

That's how it was with the apostles. They had a lot of work to do every day. They tried to help all the people. They finally decided that they needed help to take care of them all.

"What should we do?" they asked. "It's not right for us to stop teaching about Jesus." Then they got an idea. "Let's choose seven men who love Jesus to help all these new followers." Everyone liked the idea. So they chose seven men to be the apostles' helpers.

Four of the seven men they chose had "different-sounding" names. But three had names like boys have today. Their names were Stephen, Philip and Nicolas.

The apostles stopped to pray for the seven new helpers before they went to work.

Questions:

1. Who needed help caring for the new Jesus followers? (the apostles)

2. How many men did they choose to be helpers? (seven)

Activity:

Name the three new helpers mentioned in the story (Stephen, Philip and Nicolas). Do you have any friends by that name? Let's pray for them today. (See prayer below.)

Prayer:

Dear God, when the apostles needed help, You chose seven men to help with the work. You cared about the apostles, the new Jesus' followers, and the seven men. You care about my friend, _____, too. Please help him(her) today. Amen.

WALKING HOME
ACTS 6:6

Pray for each other. James 5:16

Linda and her friend, Jeannie, walked home from school every day. They always walked past the old church and around the corner toward home. They liked to walk together. But today they were not having fun. The "big" girls from the fifth grade class were following them.

"Baby! Baby! Linda is a baby! Jeannie is a baby!" the big girls yelled. They ran up behind them. Then they pushed them. "See these rocks? Tomorrow we're going to throw them at you. You'll cry like babies then," they laughed as they ran away.

Linda thought a minute. Then she said, "Let's go to my house and talk to my mom." They ran all the way and burst through the door.

When Linda's mom saw them, she said, "Hey! What's wrong?" Linda and Jeannie sat down and told her everything. "Well," said Mom, "I don't want you to get hurt. Let's see. Maybe I should talk to the girls or to the teachers. But, first, let's pray." So she reached out to put her arms around Linda and Jeannie.

"Dear God, please keep Linda and Jeannie safe," prayed Mom, "and help the fifth grade girls to stop bothering them. Help me, too, when I talk to the girls and the teachers. Thank You for Your help. Amen."

_____, Linda, Jeannie and Mom prayed together when they had a problem. We can do that, too.

Questions:
1. Why were Linda and Jeannie "scared"? (The big girls called them names, and said they'd throw rocks at them.)
2. What did Mom do with Linda and Jeannie right then? (prayed)

Activity:
Write the names of your family on this page. Ask God to help each person at work, school, home or wherever they are.

Prayer:
Dear God, please help _____, _____, _____, and me today (or tonight). Thank You. Amen.

WHO'S IN THE CHARIOT?
ACTS 8:26-40

Make followers of all people in the world. *Matthew 28:19*

_____, have you ever talked to a person who was from a different country? Where was the person from? Was he on a trip when you talked with him?

One day Philip talked to a man from a different place. Let's hear a story about Philip and this man.

An angel of God had come to Philip. "Go down that road," the angel said. So Philip did what God's angel said. On that road he saw a man from Ethiopia. The man was a leader of the people in Ethiopia. He was on a trip. This day he sat in his chariot. (A chariot is like a big wagon pulled by horses.) He was reading the Bible.

God's Spirit said, "Philip, go over to the man's chariot."

So Philip ran over to stand by the chariot. He listened. The man was reading about Jesus.

"Do you know what you're reading?" asked Philip.

"No," said the man. "I wish someone would tell me what it means."

So Philip told him about Jesus. "Jesus is God's Son," Philip said. "He died and came back to life."

The man believed Philip was telling him the truth, and he said, "I want to be baptized like Jesus was." So the man from Ethiopia became a Jesus follower.

At first, Philip did not know why the angel told him to go down that road. But, Philip did it anyway. Philip was glad that he did what the angel said because the man from Ethiopia learned about Jesus!

We will always be glad when we do what God tells us to do.

Questions:
1. Who told Philip to go down that road? (an angel)
2. Who did Philip see on the road? (an Ethiopian man reading the Bible)
2. Did the man from Ethiopia believe in Jesus? (yes)

Activities:
1. Pretend to ride in a chariot. Lead the horses over the rocky road.
2. Draw a picture of a chariot. (See explanation in story.)

Prayer:
Dear God, would You please help me to share with others what I am learning about You in these stories? Amen.

A BRIGHT LIGHT
ACTS 9:1-9, 11, 12

If anyone belongs to Christ, then he is made new. 2 Corinthians 5:17

A long time ago there lived a man who hated all the people who loved and followed Jesus. His name was Saul.

One day Saul was on his way to find the "Jesus followers." He wanted to throw them in jail. As he walked on the road to the city of Damascus, a light came down from the sky. It flashed all around him! The light shone so brightly that Saul fell to the ground. Then a voice said, "Saul, why are you hurting me?"

"Who are you?" Saul asked.

"I am Jesus. You hurt me when you put my followers in jail. Get up and go into the city. Wait there until I tell you what to do next."

When Saul stood up, he tried to look around him. But he could not see! (_____, close your eyes. Isn't it a funny feeling to see only darkness? It must have been a funny feeling for Saul, too.)

His friends led him by the hand to the house of a man named Judas. Saul stayed there for three days. He did not eat or drink. Saul prayed and waited for God to tell him what to do next.

The bright light got Saul's attention so Jesus could talk to him. God wanted to change Saul's ideas and actions. When Saul decided to believe and follow Jesus, then God made him new on the inside. God will do that for us, too. To be new on the inside means to want to love and not hate; share and not steal; tell the truth and not lie. But most of all it means that we believe and love Jesus.

Questions:
1. What flashed all around Saul? (a bright light)
2. Did Saul change his ideas about Jesus? (yes)

Activities:
1. Shine a flashlight or a lamp without a shade on your child.
2. Play the blindfold game. Blindfold one person. Another person leads him around. (The blindfolded person must trust the leader not to lead him astray.) Take turns with your child playing this game.

Prayer:
Dear God, You helped Saul decide to change his ideas and actions. Help me to listen and obey when You want to change my ideas and actions. Please make me new on the inside. Amen.

DECIDING TO FOLLOW JESUS
ACTS 9:10-22

Jesus said, "Follow me." *Matthew 9:9*

_____, what would you do if someone did not like you and wanted to hurt you? You would probably want to stay as far away from him as possible, wouldn't you? That is just how Ananias felt.

Ananias was God's friend and a follower of Jesus. God told him to go visit the blinded Saul. "Lord, I've heard many bad things about this man," Ananias said. "He hurts the Jesus followers and puts them in jail."

"Saul is changing," said God. "I want Saul to tell lots of people about Jesus. Go, now. And don't worry."

Blind Saul was alone, hungry, and tired when Ananias saw him. Ananias touched Saul and said, "Jesus told me to come talk to you." Right away Saul could see again!

Saul was a new Jesus follower. He decided to believe God's words about Jesus.

To decide means to make up your mind. We can make up our minds to believe and follow Jesus, too.

Questions:

1. Who told Ananias to go see Saul? (God)

2. Who decided to follow Jesus? (Saul)

Activities:

1. Try to draw a picture with your eyes closed.

2. Count how many meals you would miss if you did not eat for three days (three breakfasts, three lunches, three dinners = nine meals). Saul did not eat for three days.

Prayer:

Dear God, Saul decided to follow Jesus. Ananias followed You even when he was afraid. I want to follow Jesus, too. Teach me more about being Your follower. Amen.

SAUL STAYS SAFE
ACTS 9:22-25

The Lord protects those who truly believe. *Psalm 31:23*

_____, listen to a story about how God kept Saul safe. God had a very special plan for Saul. No one ever could stop God's plan. God wanted Saul to tell lots of people how to be a follower of Jesus.

But there were some men who got very mad about this plan. These men did not follow or believe Jesus. They wanted to find Saul and get rid of him. Every day, they watched where he went. Every night they planned to catch him. But Saul heard about this awful plan. God helped Saul get away from these men.

One night, Saul's friends came to him and said, "Tonight is the night. We will sneak you out of the city. Then you will be safe."

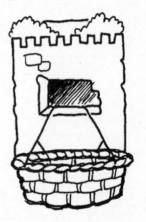

So Saul said good-bye to his friends. Then he climbed into a big basket. His friends put the basket (with Saul inside) through a hole in the city wall. On the other side of the wall he was safe from the angry men.

God protected Saul. God will keep us safe, also.

Questions:
1. What was God's plan for Saul? (He wanted Saul to tell lots of people about Jesus.)
2. What was the plan of the men who were against Saul? (to get rid of Saul)
3. How did God save Saul? (Some of Saul's friends sneaked him out of the city in a basket.)

Activities:
1. Get a clothes basket or container. Let your child climb into it and imagine what it felt like to go through the hole in the wall.
2. Put a doll or stuffed animal into a basket and lift it over a chair.

Prayer:
Dear God, You kept Saul safe from the angry men. I know You will keep me safe, too. Amen.

THE PEACEMAKER
ACTS 9:26-31

Those who work to bring peace are happy. *Matthew 5:9*

_____, how do you feel when you tell the truth, but the other children say you are lying? You want people to believe you when you talk to them, don't you? So did Saul.

Saul had come to the city of Jerusalem. He wanted to meet the Jesus followers there. But they would not believe that he had changed. They were afraid of him. They thought he was lying. He felt sad.

Then a man named Barnabas saw what was happening. He wanted to help Saul and the followers of Jesus in Jerusalem. So he took Saul by the arm and brought him to the apostles (the leaders of the Jesus followers).

Barnabas said, "Saul is *really* telling the truth. He *has* changed. Saul is a Jesus follower, now. And he wants to be our friend."

Barnabas helped Saul and the others to understand and believe each other. Barnabas was a peacemaker, a helper, and a friend.

Questions:
1. What happened when Saul came to Jerusalem? (The Jesus followers didn't believe Saul had changed. They thought he was lying.)
2. Who helped Saul and the Jesus followers to understand each other? (Barnabas)

Activities:
1. Name some ways that your child can be a peacemaker, helper, or friend (ideas: help brothers and sisters to understand each other; share toys; if a playmate is making fun of another, "stand up" for them).

2. Parents, put stickers or stars on this page when your child tries to be a peacemaker . . . today or tomorrow. (Use a red pencil or crayon to draw the stars if you do not have stickers.)

Prayer:
Dear God, I know that You are the one who helps to bring real peace and understanding. Help me to be Your peacemaker. Thank You. Amen.

THE SEWING LADY
ACTS 9:36-43

Many believed in the Lord. Acts 9:42

_____, has anyone ever made you a shirt or maybe a jacket or a pair of pants? Who sewed it for you?

A long time ago a lady named Tabitha sewed shirts and jackets for her many friends. Tabitha was a follower of Jesus. She liked to help the poor people. But one day she got very sick and died. All of her friends were very sad. They missed her.

When her friends learned that Peter was in a city close by, they called him. "Please, Peter," they said, "hurry and come."

They took him upstairs when he got to the house. All the people were crying. They showed Peter all the coats and shirts and pants that Tabitha had made for them.

Peter said, "Everyone, please leave the room." Then he knelt down and prayed to God. After he prayed, he said, "Tabitha, stand up!" Slowly, she opened her eyes. Then she sat up! Peter took her hand and helped her stand up. "Alright," he said, "you may all come back into the room."

"She's alive!" they said. "Our friend, Tabitha, is alive!"

When the good news about Tabitha, the sewing lady, spread all over the town, many people believed and followed Jesus.

Questions:

1. Who did Tabitha's friends call when she died? (Peter)

2. What did Peter do after the people left the room? (prayed to God)

3. Did Tabitha come back to life? (yes)

Activities:

1. If you sew, show your child. Allow him(her) to help.

2. Show your child a sewing kit with needle and thread.

Prayer:

Dear Jesus, many people believed in You when they heard the Good News. I pray that many people will believe in You today when they hear the Good News. Amen.

BILLY
ACTS 10:34-43

To God all men are the same. Galatians 2:6

"It's stopped raining now, Billy," said Mom. "You can put on your boots and coat and go outside to play."

"Oh, yah!" yelled Billy, as he grabbed his coat. Then he got quiet. "But I don't have anyone to play with. That's no fun. He thought for a minute. "Will you come play with me, Mom?"

"Maybe I will later, Billy," said Mom. "But why don't you go next door and ask Carlos to play?"

Billy whined, "M-o-m, Carlos talks funny, and he looks different. Anyway, there's something wrong with his arm."

"I know, Billy," said Mom, "but you might be surprised. Maybe the two of you would have fun together."

Slowly, Billy walked into his bedroom. He saw his baseball under the bed. "Carlos can't even throw a baseball," he thought. "B-u-t, maybe he can learn." Billy sat quietly on the floor. "The other night in our bedtime story, I learned that every person is the same to God. God doesn't care if a boy has different skin or a funny-looking arm."

Billy jumped up, grabbed his baseball, and ran into the kitchen. "Mom!" he yelled. "I think I'll go ask Carlos if he wants to play."

Mom smiled as Billy raced out the front door.

Questions:

1. How was Carlos different from Billy? (He talked different, looked different, and had something wrong with his arm.)

2. Does it matter to God what color your skin is or where you come from? (no)

Activity:

Draw a picture of a boy or a girl in a wheelchair, or an old person, or a blind man, or a child of a different race.

Prayer:

Dear God, thank You for loving and treating all people the same. Amen.

A NICKNAME FOR JESUS' FOLLOWERS
Acts 11:19-25

In Antioch the followers were
called Christians for the first time. *Acts 11:26*

A nickname is a different, sometimes shorter, name that people call you. _____, do you have a nickname? (A boy named Joseph might be nickname "Joe," a short boy named William might be called "Shorty.")

The people in the city of Antioch had a nickname for the followers of Jesus. The nickname was "Christian." They were called "Christians" because they loved, believed, and followed Christ Jesus.

When people who did not love Jesus began hurting Jesus' followers, many of the Jesus followers moved to other cities. When each Christian got to a new town, he talked about Jesus. Many new people decided to follow Jesus.

The city of Antioch had lots of new Jesus followers. They needed a leader so a man named Barnabas came to help. "I have a man I want you to meet," Barnabas told his friends. "His name is Paul. He used to be called Saul, but since he decided to follow Jesus, we call him Paul. Please be his friend."

For the next year, Paul and Barnabas stayed in Antioch and taught the new Christians.

Questions:
1. What was the nickname given to Jesus' followers? (Christian)
2. What was Saul's other name? (Paul)

Activities:
1. Underline the word "Christ" in the word "Christian."
2. Name your family members' nicknames (examples: Beth for Elizabeth, Gramps for Grandpa, Sissy for sister).

Prayer:
Dear Jesus, I am a Christian because I love, believe, and follow You. I like to be called by that nickname. Amen.

PETER AND THE ANGEL
ACTS 12:1-12

I can lie down and go to sleep. And I will wake up again
because the Lord protects me. *Psalm 3:5*

Peter was a good man. He talked to others about his friend, Jesus.
Many people liked Peter. But mean King Herod Agrippa did not like
Peter. He did not even like Jesus. So the king grabbed Peter and threw
him in jail.

The jail was not a nice place. It was dirty. Peter had heavy chains
on his feet and hands. Sixteen big soldier-men stayed around Peter so
he could not get away.

But, _____, guess what? Peter was brave. Re-
member, he had the courage of the Holy Spirit. "God will take care of
me," he thought. "So I'll close my eyes and go to sleep."

During the night, while Peter was sleeping, he felt someone touch
his side. When he opened his eyes, he saw an ANGEL! "Hurry,
Peter!" said the angel. "Let's go!"

Right away, the chains fell off Peter's hands and feet. God opened
the jail door for Peter and the angel to walk out.

It was just like Peter thought before he fell asleep. God took care of
Peter. And God will take care of us, too.

Questions:
    1. Who woke Peter up? (an angel)
    2. Did God take care of Peter? (yes)
Activities:
    1. Count to sixteen. (There were sixteen
soldier-men guarding Peter in the jail.)
    2. Point to the angel in the picture.
    3. Close your eyes and pretend to go to
sleep. (Make a pretend "snore" sound.)
Prayer:
    Dear God, You helped Peter when he
needed it. I believe You will help me, too.
So I will go to sleep peacefully. Amen.

KNOCK-KNOCK! WHO'S THERE?
ACTS 12:10-16

You hear our prayers. You answer us in amazing ways. *Psalm 65:2, 5*

When Peter followed the angel out of the jail, the sixteen big soldier-men did not stop them. They walked out the door and down the street. Then zap! The angel was gone. Peter stood alone in the middle of the road. It was night time. And it was very dark.

"God sent the angel to help me get out of jail. God took care of me then, and I know He will take care of me now," whispered Peter.

Peter walked down the road in the dark until he came to a friend's house. Many of Jesus' followers were there, praying. Peter knocked on the door. "Who's there?" asked a young girl named Rhoda.

"Please open the door, Rhoda," answered Peter. Rhoda was so excited to hear Peter's voice that she forgot to open the door. She ran to tell the others. But they did not believe her. They just kept praying.

Finally they opened the door. "It *is* Peter!" they shouted. God has answered our prayers."

_____, do you think Peter's friends were happy to see him?

Questions:

1. Where did Peter go after God sent the angel to get him out of jail? (to a friend's house)

2. Who forgot to open the door so Peter could come inside? (a young girl named Rhoda)

Activities:

1. Play a knock-knock joke or game.

2. Talk about a time when God answered your prayer and it surprised you.

Prayer:

Dear God, You always hear our prayers. Sometimes You answer in ways that surprise us. Thank You for always listening and for answering. Amen.

NIGHT TIME
PSALM 63:6-8; ACTS 12:10, 11

Lord, I remember you at night. *Psalm 119:55*

"Janey, it's almost time to get your pajamas on and brush your teeth," said Dad. Janey and her cousin, Danielle, were coloring together.

Janey looked up. "I don't want to get my pajamas on. I don't want to brush my teeth. And I don't want to go to sleep," she cried.

"What's wrong, Janey?" Danielle asked. "Are you afraid?"

Janey was quiet a minute. Then she whispered, "Yes, sometimes I *am* afraid. I don't like the dark."

After they finished coloring, they walked upstairs to Janey's room. Danielle sat down on the bed next to Janey and told her this story.

"There once was a little girl who was very afraid. She was afraid of spiders and bugs. She was afraid of thunder and lightning. But most of all she was afraid of going to sleep at night. 'What can help me?' she thought. 'Who can help me?'

"One night her mom said, 'Maybe God can help you not to be afraid. Let's ask Him.'

"So the little girl prayed, 'God, I feel afraid now. But please help me to be brave. Help me to go to sleep without crying.' Soon the little girl fell asleep.

"The next day her Sunday-school teacher showed her some Bible verses. 'Even at night, I feel His leading. Because He is close by my side, I will not be hurt. I go to bed and sleep in peace. Lord, only You keep me safe. At night I have a song and I pray to my living God.'

That night the little girl prayed again. She sang a song. And then she went to sleep for the second night in a row.

"Janey, that little girl was ME," said Danielle. "God helped me. He'll help you, too."

Questions:
   1. Who was afraid to go to sleep at night? (Janey and Danielle)
   2. Did God help them? (yes)

Activity:
   Color together.

Prayer:
   Dear God, please help me go to sleep peacefully. Amen.

THE TRAVELING MAN
ACTS 18:1-10

Because of his (Paul's) work, every Jew and Greek in the country of Asia heard the word of the Lord. *Acts 19:10*

_____, do you like to go on trips? Paul went on many trips. He was a traveling man. Everywhere he went he told people the good news about Jesus.

When you come to a new city, where do you stop first? Do you stop at the gas station? Do you go to the motel? Do you stop to eat in a restaurant? Where do you think Paul went?

When Paul got to a new city, he went to the Temple-church. He told the people about Jesus. Some believed him and some did not. Some people prayed with him and some wanted to hurt him.

One night, Paul had a dream. God talked to Paul in this dream. He said, "Don't be afraid! Keep talking to the people about me. Remember, I am with you!

So Paul kept telling people that Jesus was alive. When people did not believe, Paul said, "I am telling the truth. But I cannot make you believe. You have to make up your own mind."

Just like Paul, we have friends that we wish would believe in Jesus. We can pray for them. We can read a Jesus story to them. We can tell them that God loves them. But we cannot decide for them. They have to make up their own mind.

Questions:
1. Who went on many trips? (Paul)
2. Did Paul tell people about Jesus? (yes)
3. Did Paul *make* people believe in Jesus? (no)

Activity:
Pretend to drive your car on a trip, stopping to get gas or food.

Prayer:
Dear God, please help me not to be afraid to talk about You to my friends. Then would You please help my friends to decide to believe in Jesus? Amen.

A SCARY STORM
ACTS 27:7-42

When you pass through the waters, I (God) will be with you.

Isaiah 43:2

_____, can you name some things that happen when a storm comes? (pause for response) A springtime storm brings clouds, rain, wind, thunder, and lightning. Have you ever been on a boat when a storm came up? Paul was.

Paul and 275 men were on a sailing trip. They sailed slowly because the wind was blowing so hard. Every day the wind blew harder. Paul said, "I think a very big storm is coming. Maybe we should stop." But they would not listen to Paul. They just kept on sailing.

The wind blew for many days. They could not see the sun or stars. It was so cloudy! It rained hard. The wind beat against the boat. "We're going to die!" the men cried. They were too scared and sick to even eat.

But one night an angel from God came to Paul. "Don't be afraid!" he said. "You will have a boat crash, but God will save all 276 men. Believe me. I am telling the truth." So Paul told the men what the angel said. He found some food, thanked God for it, and began to eat. When the men saw Paul eating, they decided to eat, also. It was the first time they had eaten in fourteen days. Soon they all felt much better.

The next morning the boat hit a big rock. CRASH! It could not move! The winds smashed against the boat. The big waves broke the boat into pieces.

So all the men jumped into the water. Some swam to the land. Others floated on the broken pieces of boat. But they *all* were safe just like God said they would be.

Paul was thankful and happy. So were the men. God had kept them safe in the scary storm.

Questions:
1. Who sailed in a boat? (Paul and 275 men)
2. Did God keep them safe in the storm? (yes)

Activities:
1. Make blowing sounds like the wind.
2. Draw a picture of the boat with a sail.

Prayer:
Dear God, please keep my family and me safe when a storm comes. Thank You. Amen.

THE PIGGY BANK
2 CORINTHIANS 8:1-15; 9:1-15

What you have can help others who are in need. *2 Corinthians 8:14*

Carl walked into the kitchen and saw his Dad sitting at the table listening to the radio. He seemed sad. Carl heard the voice on the radio saying words like "storm," "winds," "crying," "hurt," and "hospital."

"What is he saying, Daddy?" asked Carl.

"There has been a big storm in a far away place. Houses have been crashed, cars are wrecked, people are hurt and some have died," said Dad.

"I want to help them," said Carl. "Can we do that?"

"Well, I don't know," said Dad. "Do you have any ideas?"

"How about if we send them some money," said Carl. "They must not have any food or clothes if their houses got crashed."

"Good idea!" said Dad.

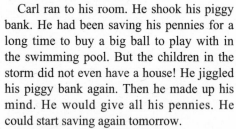

Carl ran to his room. He shook his piggy bank. He had been saving his pennies for a long time to buy a big ball to play with in the swimming pool. But the children in the storm did not even have a house! He jiggled his piggy bank again. Then he made up his mind. He would give all his pennies. He could start saving again tomorrow.

Carl and his dad talked about it with the whole family. They all decided to give some of what they had to the poor hurting people in the storm.

God is happy when we give to people in need.

Questions:

1. What happened in the far away place? (a storm crashed people's houses, etc.)

2. Who wanted to help? (Carl)

Activity:

Plan a giving project as a family (ideas: the city food shelf, the Red Cross, a church missionary fund). Follow through.

Prayer:

Dear God, help our family as we give to _____ (name the project you mentioned in the activity). Thank You. Amen.

108

NO SPAGHETTI DINNER
EPHESIANS 6:1-4

Children, obey your parents. *Colossians 3:20*

Carrie ran into the house. She was out of breath from running so hard. "Lori wants me to come over and play on her new swing set. Can I go? Please! Can I? Can I?" The words tumbled out of Carrie's mouth.

"Dinner will be ready to eat in a little while," said Dad. "You can go next door to Lori's house, but come home when I call you."

Fifteen minutes before dinner time, Dad leaned out the window and called to Carrie. "Come in, Carrie, it's almost time to eat." But Carrie acted like she did not hear her dad. A few minutes later, Dad called again. But, just like before, Carrie did not listen. So Mom and Dad and brother Tom sat down to eat.

Just as they finished dinner, Carrie walked in the front door. "I'm hungry," she said. "Is it time to eat?"

"We are finished eating," Dad said sadly. "We had spaghetti. But it's all gone now."

"Oh, no!" said Carrie. Spaghetti was her favorite. Tears rolled down her cheeks. "I wish I had come home when you called. I'm sorry."

"I know you are, Carrie." Mom hugged her sad little girl. Carrie sat down at the table to eat a sandwich. Then she remembered the Bible verse she learned at church school: "Children, obey your parents."

_____, God is happy when boys and girls do what their parents tell them to do.

Questions:
1. Did Carrie obey her parents? (no)
2. Was Carrie sorry? (yes)

Activities:
1. Name your favorite dinner food.
2. PARENTS: Put stars on this page to-morrow when your child obeys.

Prayer:
Dear God, please help me obey Mom and Dad. Thank You. Amen.

TIMOTHY'S LETTER
2 TIMOTHY 1:3-7; 2:15; 3:15-17; 4:6-8, 17

I always remember you in my prayers. *2 Timothy 1: 3*

_____, have you ever had a letter come just to you? It was very special, wasn't it? Timothy had a letter come just to him. It was very special to him. The letter was from Paul. Paul was like Timothy's "adopted" dad. He loved Paul. And Paul loved Timothy.

Paul wrote the letter to Timothy while in jail. He was all alone. He missed Timothy so much. The people in Rome were very mad at him for talking about Jesus. They wanted "old man Paul" to die. Paul knew that soon he would go to heaven to be with Jesus.

So Paul sat on the cold floor of the jail and wrote to Timothy.

"Dear Timothy,
I always pray for you. How I wish to see you again! I know your mom and grandma taught you to love God when you were a little boy. Remember: God is not the one who makes us afraid. God is the one who makes us brave. Study the Bible. Its words are true. My life is almost over, but I know that I have done what God wanted me to do. Sometimes people have been mean to me. But God has always been with me. Please hurry and come see me here in jail.
Love, Paul"

Paul's letter was very special to Timothy. He probably read it many times. We can read it, too, because it is written down in the Bible.

Question:
Where was Paul when he wrote the letter to Timothy? (in jail)
Activity:
Write a letter to someone that you do not see very often.
Prayer:
Dear God, I pray for _____ today. Please help him(her) to know that You love him(her). Amen. (Fill in the blank with the name of the person to whom you wrote the letter.)

WHAT DID YOU SAY?
JAMES 1:19; 3:1-12; 5:12

Praises and curses come from the same mouth!
My brothers, this should not happen. *James 3:10*

_____, when Jesus was growing up here on earth He lived with His mom and dad, Mary and Joseph, and His brothers and sisters. One of Jesus' brothers was named James. When James grew up, he believed that Jesus was God's Son. He knew his father, Joseph, was Jesus' adopted dad. James wrote one of the books in the Bible. In that book he said to be careful about how we talk. Listen to a story about how one little boy and his family were not careful about what they said:

Willie went with his mom and dad to church one Sunday morning. They went into the big room and sat down together. They prayed to God. "Praise the Lord! Praise the Lord!" they sang. As they walked to the car, Willie said, "Bobby is a dumbhead! He tore up the picture I colored. I hate him."

Then they all got into the car. They drove down the road and started to turn at the next street. But just then another car moved in front of them. They almost had a wreck!

"How stupid!" said Willie's dad. "He must not have a brain!"

James said that "praises" and "curses" sometimes come from the same mouth. He also said, "This should not happen. You hurt the people that God made when you 'curse' them. God made people to be like himself. So be careful what you say about the people God made."

Questions:

1. What was Jesus' brother's name? (James)

2. What did James say we should be careful about? (what we say)

Activity:

Name bad and good ways to use our tongues (ideas: bad—lying, calling people bad names; good—singing, praying, saying thank you).

Prayer:

Dear God, please help me to be careful about what I say. Amen.

IS JESUS COMING BACK?
REVELATION 21:1-7, 22-27; 22:20

Yes, I am coming soon. *Revelation 22:20*

_____, what did God make in the very beginning? Yes, He made the heavens or sky. And He made the earth with its grass and trees and flowers. He made Adam and Eve and all the people.

Then God sent Jesus as a baby. (He was born at Christmas time.) Jesus grew up, died, and came back alive. When He left to go back to live with God, His Father, He said, "Some day I will come back."

He has not done that yet. We do not know when that will be. But it will happen! Jesus *will* come back! And He'll make a new earth. He will be King. He will be the best King that there has ever been. All people will get down on their knees and bow to Jesus. After that there will be no other kings.

For all people who love God and believe in Jesus, there will be no more fighting. There will be no more sickness or hurt. No one will ever cry again. And guess what? There will not even be any night time. (You will never have to go to sleep in the dark again.)

God is the only one who knows when this will happen. It may be a long time from now or it may be a short time.

But it will happen! This is the best news! Jesus is coming back!

Questions:
1. Who was born at Christmas time? (Jesus)
2. Where is Jesus now? (in heaven with God)
3. Is Jesus coming back? (yes)

Activities:
1. Name kinds of good news (ideas: your birthday; grandma is coming; we're going to the park, etc.).
2. Name the best news ever. (Jesus is coming back.)
3. Make a colorful poster with these words. Display it in your room.

Jesus is coming back. That is good news! I do not know ...appen. But I know it is true. Amen.